WE,
THE
OTHERS

.ll.

WE, THE OTHERS

Allophones, Immigrants, and Belonging in Canada

TOULA DRIMONIS

Edited by Leila Marshy
Prepared for the press by Elise Moser, Kaiya Cade Smith Blackburn
Cover design: Leila Marshy, Debbie Geltner

Cover image: Courtesy of the author: Peter Drimonis in his first restaurant, Le Coin Blanc, at the corner of Henri-Julien and Mont-Royal Streets, Montreal
Author photo: Janice Lawandi

Library and Archives Canada Cataloguing in Publication

Title: We, the others: allophones, immigrants, and belonging in Canada / by Toula Drimonis.
Names: Drimonis, Toula, author.
Identifiers: Canadiana (print) 20220206449 | Canadiana (ebook) 20220206953 | ISBN 9781773901213 (softcover) | ISBN 9781773901220 (HTML) | ISBN 9781773901237 (PDF)
Subjects: LCSH: Immigrants—Canada—Social conditions. | LCSH: Canada—Emigration and immigration—Social aspects. | LCSH: Canada—Emigration and immigration—Government policy. | LCSH: Emigration and immigration law—Social aspects—Canada. | LCSH: Canada—Race relations. | LCSH: Canada—Ethnic relations. | LCSH: Immigrants—Canada—Public opinion. | LCSH: Canada—Emigration and immigration—Public opinion.
Classification: LCC JV7225.2 .D75 2022 | DDC 305.9/069120971—dc23

Printed and bound in Canada.

The publisher gratefully acknowledges the support of the Government of Canada through the Canada Council for the Arts, the Canada Book Fund, and of the Government of Quebec through the Société de développement des entreprises culturelles (SODEC) and the Programme de credit d'impôt pour l'édition de livres—Gestion SODEC.

Linda Leith Publishing
Montreal
www.lindaleith.com

Advance praise for *We, the Others*

"When I completed this book and laid it down, the first word that came to me was insightful. As an Indigenous person who has been often caught in the Anglo-Québécois divide, having profound relationships on both sides, Drimonis's contribution is both significant and a gift."

> —The Honourable Romeo Saganash, former federal MP, Cree lawyer, and Quebec's first Indigenous Member of Parliament.

"Imagine my astonishment when I discovered that Toula, a Greek first-generation immigrant to Quebec and Canada, GETS me, a Black Canadian Québécoise woman of diverse ethnic origins! Her descriptions of the overlapping layers of identities that sit alongside our love for the French language, culture and democratic social norms struck a chord in my heart and soul. Toula understands how immigrants both knowingly and unknowingly absorb the heart of Quebec culture while simultaneously recognizing a Canadian identity, which is then again stacked upon other identities. This book is a MUST READ for all. It will enrich one's understanding of the immigrant experience and that of integration through the multiple stages. Thank you, Toula."

> —The Honourable Marlene Jennings, former federal MP, first Black woman from Quebec to be elected to Parliament, former Chair of the Quebec Community Groups Network.

"*We, the Others* is a beautiful paean to Toula Drimonis's Greek immigrant parents, and to all immigrant parents like hers. Drimonis evokes a respect for ordinary people who work hard every day, build a life for their families, and who are like every Canadian or Quebecer—save for the upheaval, fear, and precariousness of escaping conflict or poverty and starting anew.

We, the Others makes a strong case in favour of immigration and tells us how newcomers make us richer in every way. Thanks to immigrants, we discover new ideas, languages, foods, and cultures without going much further than the local dépanneur. As Drimonis notes, every new wave changes us imperceptibly until, over time, the *others* are now simply us, and we are all the better for it."

—Michael Fukushima, Canadian filmmaker, former head NFB Animation Studio, director of *Minoru: Memory of Exile*, an animated documentary about the Japanese-Canadian internment.

"*We, the Others* is a riveting story that reveals a deep understanding of Canadian history, cultural norms, struggles of immigrant communities, and how communities are woven together by a shared yearning to survive and thrive. Toula does not shy away from shedding light on our country's racist past and present, and does so with bravery and an unapologetic sense of pride. Her words are real, raw and lay bare truths that many of us have lived."

—Fariha Naqvi Mohamed, Canadian journalist and columnist; the first woman to wear the hijab on Quebec television in her role as a video journalist for CityNews Montreal.

"Toula takes us on an adventure of a lifetime. From her parents' departure from Greece to her unique journey growing up as a child of immigrants, through to her extensive work as a journalist and keen observer of Quebec society, she describes the challenges of integration against the backdrop of hardships and disappointments that many immigrants face while trying to thrive in a society that continues to view them as a threat to their language, economic growth and security."

—The Honourable Eleni Bakopanos, former federal MP, first Greek-born woman elected to Parliament.

Για εσένα, μπαμπά

Question: How are we supposed to treat others?
Answer: There are no others.

—Ramana Maharishi

Contents

Introduction

It's early October in Neapoli, a small coastal town in southern Greece. Though it is still gorgeous and warm, most of the tourists have left and the waterfront businesses once again serve only locals. I'm sipping an iced frappé coffee while a group of older men, the town priest among them, slam tiles on a backgammon board in a nearby café.

All this is so familiar. I spent every summer here as a teenager, swimming, suntanning, and reading. Languid days that stretched on forever. This feels as much like home as sitting by the Lachine Canal in Montreal.

Much has changed over the years, of course. Modern hotels have sprouted in the seaside town, new cafés and restaurants line the waterfront, and the kids I used to bump into now have children of their own. The main pier no longer welcomes the small fishing boats that used to return early every morning with the daily catch. Nowadays, they go to a smaller pier further south, removed from the town's hustle and bustle. The local elementary school has been painted in beautiful pastel colours and the basketball court by the beach, where I used to shoot hoops, is far nicer than I remember. But mostly, it's still the same. The sun still sets on the same sweet spot in the ocean, then bursts into flames near the island of Elafonisos. The pier still welcomes shuffling, elderly walkers and lanky teenagers up to no good. Fishermen still watch their rods for hours, oblivious to the noise behind them, and boats still bob up and down in the distance as the waves roll in.

Neapoli is the town my dad walked to as a 14-year-old to sell oranges from the family grove. He got up in the middle of the night and followed a well-laden donkey on the rugged paths over the mountains to the town's weekend market. It was dark out, there were no lights, and he couldn't see, but—as he told me every time I asked—the donkey knew the way. He would simply grab its tail and follow. He arrived just in time for the bustling Saturday morning market and left only when the oranges had been sold. He often bartered for peanuts or fish or whatever else was plentiful. It seemed such a far-fetched tale that, even while quite young, I had to check with aunts and uncles to confirm it was true.

When my father first arrived in Canada, he had fifty dollars in his pocket. He had paid for the suit he was wearing with a small loan he needed to repay as soon as possible. At his first job as a dishwasher, the sign above the sink was as laconic as his Spartan heritage: "*You break a dish I break your head.*"

The price for this chance at the promised land? Eighteen-hour workdays and hands soaked in kitchen grease. My father was hot-tempered and proud. I imagine him absorbing insults and petty power trips with just one goal in mind: to save and save and save until he could open his own restaurant. That was the only way he could shape the future to his liking and start a family of his own. There were hundreds of thousands of men like him all across North America.

Years later, he returned to Neapoli to buy a summer home for his family. It was an unspoken tribute to the penniless teenager he had been when he first set foot here, and a proud testament to the affluent middle-class man he had become.

It can sometimes be hard to wrap my brain around the fact that I'm only one generation removed from poverty so desperate that a young boy had to crisscross mountains in the dead of night to sell fruit. I marvel at the ingenuity and determination of people like him with limited education, limited means, limited opportunities—and boundless aspirations. I marvel at their willingness to create something out of nothing. The obstacles they faced, the way they navigated their struggles with quiet dignity and purpose. How they built something that could contain not just the old country, but the new life they would construct for themselves, their kids, and generations to come.

I think about them every time politicians and pundits talk about immigrants as a financial burden and a threat to "our" way of life. Or when newcomers are treated only as a means to an end, an opportunity to fill temporary labour needs. The very people who know nothing about the upheaval and the challenges of migration feel entitled to offer solutions and opinions on how best to integrate migrants.

For me, immigration isn't an abstract concept discussed within the walls of an ivory tower. When I think of immigration, I see the faces of my father, my mother, my aunts and uncles; family and friends who worked in restaurant kitchens, factories, and taxicabs. Immigration is personal to me.

Ὅπου γη και πατρίς (*Opou gi kai patris*). Wherever there is land, there is a country. Old-school Greek immigrants sometimes mutter that to themselves in a fatalistic, slightly resigned tone. It is an acknowledgment of a truth and all the concessions that come with it. Wherever there is land, there is a country. Any country can become your country. You can uproot yourself and find soil elsewhere and start over. You can even bloom. It's being done every day.

And, so, Quebec became my father's country. When my mother married him, it became hers, too. And, years later, after I was born in Montreal's Royal Victoria Hospital, it became mine.

In Quebec, those like me—immigrants and the children of immigrants whose first language is neither French nor English—are called "allophones." According to the 2016 Statistics Canada census, we are 13.8 percent of Quebecers and a little over 23 percent of Montrealers. To be an allophone is to have a mother tongue that is *allos* (other): a language other than French or English. It's meant as an easy way to differentiate us from francophones, the French-speaking majority, and anglophones, the English-speaking minority. Although terms such as allophones, francophones and anglophones are quickly becoming outdated, they remain part of the vernacular and will be used here for the purposes of easy identification.

Of course, there are also immigrants and second-generation children whose first language is either French or English, but most of us are "allos," grouped together as something other—*autre* in census forms. Benign as it may be, this delineates the two majority groups against which we are forever juxtaposed and measured.

Allos. It's strange to be *de facto* sidelined, to be defined by what we are assumed to be missing rather than what we bring. It's strange to be expected to sit quietly as two linguistic and cultural groups trade non-stop grievances about their colonial history and the waning dominance of their respective languages. I can't imagine how Indigenous communities must feel, hearing the French and English referred to as Canada's two founding peoples, while none of the more than seventy Aboriginal languages spoken in Canada enjoy official status and 75 percent of them are currently endangered.

With the exception of Indigenous communities, we're all immigrants to Canada, regardless of timeline. Despite this, allophones are often treated as latecomers, guests to be benevolently welcomed or "permitted." We're routinely told to "just leave" if we're unhappy or fail to display the appropriate gratitude or conformist behaviour. Yet we, too, have our grievances and fears. We, too, have a stake in every story that paints us as interlopers and threats to the dominant language and culture. And we, too, have loved ones buried in this ground.

We, the others.

I want to tell you about our stories. About my parents' story and how it shaped me. I want to demystify what it feels like to be *othered*, to be neither here nor there, to be on the outside looking in and inside looking out. To be needed yet not always wanted, to have the gift (and the burden) of perspective gained by belonging to more than one culture.

I'm here to tell you what it feels like to be a hyphenated Canadian, a Quebecer on probation, someone who is routinely called upon to prove their allegiance. I'm here to deconstruct blind spots: privilege, power and, yes, occasionally, oppression and marginalization by the majority voice. Whoever and wherever that happens to be.

I'm here to talk about *us*, for once. And it would be nice if everyone could pull up a chair and listen.

PART ONE

1. The Price of Dreams

Σαν πας στα ξέν' αγάπη μου, μην κάμεις ένα χρόνο
γιατί δεν τονε αντέχω του χωρισμού τον πόνο.
When you go off to foreign lands, my love, don't
stay a year there, because it's more than I can bear,
the pain
of separation.

—Greek folk song

I'm holding a black-and-white picture of Ourania as an eighteen-year-old bride. She is stunning, but her eyes are impossibly sad. The picture catches her staring into an unknown future. You can feel the melancholy and apprehension, the worry hanging like an invisible weight around her neck. It doesn't matter that she is excited to be getting married and leaving for a new life in Canada. This is the last time she'll be seeing her parents and her siblings, and the last time she'll be in her village, until they meet again—if they meet again. In the photograph, her brother and sisters also have long faces.

My parents' wedding pictures are celebratory but they are also steeped in sadness. Dreams come at a heavy price.

Both my father and my mother knew at a very young age that they would be leaving their homeland. Poverty and misery not only limits who you choose to be, it also requires a kind of bravery and pragmatism that can be hard for most of us to comprehend. Desperation can produce a single-mindedness that circumvents your basic needs and desires. Survival mode means that many of the cornerstones of your identity—personal interests, talents, aspirations, fears—are turned off, leaving only the essential. It's a form of self-inflicted censorship.

My parents left Greece in 1963. They boarded the TSS Olympia, a Greek Line ship, for a voyage from the port of Piraeus across the ocean to Halifax. It took them ten days to travel to Canada. Two days into the journey, my mom fell violently seasick and couldn't keep much food down. When they anchored in Italy for a while, she sampled bananas for the very first time. When they finally landed in Halifax, they were greeted as future Canadians. My mom remembers being given tea and some sort of processed cereal grains in a box as welcome gifts. Some newcomers, confusing the cereal with chicken feed, promptly threw it out. The very same day they boarded the train for Montreal, to be reunited with my father's older brother and his wife.

It was a very different time, 1963. It was a world without WhatsApp or FaceTime; where phone calls placed to the village store (as many people had no phone at home) were only for important news—deaths, marriages, births. Because international calls were a luxury and writing letters was difficult for people with limited schooling, everyday hardships, small victories, even milestones were left unshared. We can't even begin to fathom this kind of isolation anymore.

When I occasionally get aggravated at how fearful my mother sometimes is today, how she only drives on roads she knows, how she worries excessively about my safety, how she questions everything unfamiliar, I try to remember that she was once braver than I'll ever be.

My parents knew that as much as they loved their country, it couldn't sustain them. Politicians and those resistant to newcomers will talk about economic migrants as interlopers who chose to leave for greener pastures. They say, their circumstances didn't really "merit" a departure to new lands. They don't see economic migration as being as legitimate as refugees fleeing persecution and death. For some reason, economic devastation and the absence of viable prospects aren't valid reasons for seeking a better life elsewhere. As if there is a real choice to make when you are left with no choices.

"More infuriating is the word 'opportunism,' a lie created by the privileged to shame suffering strangers who crave a small taste of a decent life," writes Dina Nayeri in *The Ungrateful Refugee*. "The same hopes in their own children would be labeled 'motivation' and 'drive.'"[1]

Emerging from ten years of deadly warfare during World War II, a brutal German occupation that resulted in the deaths of thousands of Greeks from famine and mass executions, and then, in the late 1940s, a civil war that pitted friends against friends, Greece was hopelessly poor and unable to provide for a generation that longed for peace and prosperity.

---

1   Dina Nayeri, *The Ungrateful Refugee: What Immigrants Never Tell You.* (Berkeley: Catapult, 2019).

At the same time, Commonwealth countries such as Canada and Australia, enjoying the post-war economic boom, were on the hunt for new immigrants. Canada, in particular, was signalling loudly that it needed more people.[2] Thanks to bilateral agreements and international arrangements, opportunities for migrants were opening up. They started leaving home by the thousands: approximately 108,000 Greeks emigrated to Canada between 1945 and 1971. Poor and uneducated like my parents, they were close to the bottom of the social ladder and they remained there for a long time.

The southern region of Greece, where my family is from, bore the heavy brunt of this exodus. Thousands upon thousands of young men and women made up a diaspora that spilled across the world; some, never to meet again, others to find each other months or years later in the faraway country that was now their new home. Many of the villages they left behind became ghost towns as ancestral homes were abandoned. Only the cemeteries bore witness to the families that once lived there.

I grew up listening to the mournful diaspora music my parents played. The lyrics describe families split apart, mothers pining for their sons gone away on merchant ships, children working endless hours in *xenitia* (foreign lands). Even as a child, with my limited Greek, I would lie on the living room floor and listen to Stelio Kazantzidis and Grigoris Bithikotsis and feel emotions I couldn't possibly understand. Hundreds of songs have

---

2   Harold Troper, "Immigration in Canada," *The Canadian Encyclopedia*, April 22, 2013, https://www.thecanadianencyclopedia.ca/en/article/immigration.

been written about the "bitterness of exile" and "villainous foreign lands that take our best children away." Through the wailing of the bouzouki and the singer's sorrowful voice, I have felt the sadness seep into my bones.

Rebetika, the Greek blues, originated during the forced exodus of Greek refugees from Asia Minor in 1921. It is the music of the displaced, an entire musical genre created by generations of homesick people learning to navigate the culture shock of the new.

In *Nouvelles de Montréal*, a collection of short stories about Montreal, Haitian-Québécois writer Rodney Saint-Éloi describes his initial impressions of Montreal. He calls it "living in confusion."

> *J'apprends les mots pour nommer l'exil. Je suis venu ici pour apprendre. Je recompose mon visage. De nouveaux mots enrichissent mon lexique. Tuque. Mitaine. Slush. Grésil. Tempête. Pluie verglaçante … Il faut bien se couvrir pour ne pas mourir de froid.[3]*

> I'm learning the words to name the exile. I came here to learn. I recompose my face. New words enrich my vocabulary. Tuque. Mitt. Slush. Sleet. Storm. Freezing rain … You have to cover yourself well so as not to freeze to death.[4]

The words Saint-Éloi had to learn are part of a vocabulary every Quebecer knows only too well. To acquire them, to use them in a sentence, to become intimate

---

3   Rodney Saint-Éloi, "Un soir d'exile," *Nouvelles de Montréal.* (Paris: Éditions Magellan, 2018), 17.

4   Translations are by the author unless otherwise credited.

with them through repetition and sheer need is a rite of passage. They mark us as the winter-beaten inhabitants of this corner of the world.

My mother caught severe pneumonia the first winter she spent in Montreal. Having lived eighteen years of her life in southern Greece, she had no way of anticipating how harsh and inhospitable winter could be. She had barely seen snow in her life and her stylish but flimsy cream-white coat was made for mild winters in a place where almond trees blossom by February.

She had been trained as a seamstress, and Montreal had a thriving garment industry at the time, so it wasn't hard for her to find work even though she spoke neither French nor English. *Getting* to work was another story. Once she was hired for a quality-control job at a clothing factory, helping spot and repair sewing imperfections, she needed to find her way from Park Avenue and Mount Royal to a building on Bleury near De Maisonneuve. That's just a short bus ride, but she didn't trust herself to take public transit, worrying she wouldn't be able to follow instructions or explain herself if she got lost. So she walked the forty minutes each way, even as the days grew colder and the snow started falling. It is no surprise that she got sick.

My mother's stories of her first experiences navigating Montreal and working in those factories are shared by many newcomers. While exploring *Immigrec*,[5] an online oral history archive documenting the history of Greek immigration in Canada, I came across many

---

5   *Immigrec, Stories of Greek Immigration to Canada*, McGill University Greek Studies, University of Patras, York University, Simon Fraser University, 2019, https://immigrec.com/.

familiar stories of early hardship. In an audio interview a woman by the name of Chrisoula from the island of Lesbos, who now resides in Winnipeg, shares her first tentative steps working as a seamstress at a factory.

"Whatever they tell you," her husband advises before she heads out, "you'll be saying 'thank you.'"

Chrisoula can be heard explaining to the interviewer that she was ill-prepared for the job because she didn't know how to operate the electric machines.

"We didn't have any electricity in the village. I break threads, needles… Aah! Then comes the supervisor. The woman didn't say anything. She put it through, she repaired it, she gave me a little rag to make from side to side. I couldn't do any of this. She says 'Stupid! Stupid!'

'Thank you,' I responded. I didn't know what she was saying.

She was getting angrier. 'Stupid!'

'Thank you,' I continued. The more I was telling her 'thank you,' the angrier she was getting. But I didn't know."

That factory building where my mother first worked now houses the offices of the *Directeur de l'état civil*, the Quebec Director of Civil Status. Fifty-two years after she had emigrated to Montreal, she walked into that same hallway to apply for my father's death certificate—and slowly realized where she was standing. She told me about it afterwards, and I could hear the shock still in her voice. A building she had known in her early years as a young bride in Montreal with her entire life ahead of her was now the place that marked a sad new stage of her existence. Life has a way of making sure everything comes full circle—even when you don't put in the request.

My aging mother now has a proper Canadian winter coat, a sturdy pair of winter boots, and a warm pair of gloves. Defiant, however, she still refuses to wear a proper winter head covering, despite the many warm and luxurious hats my sister and I have gifted her over the years. That proud young Greek immigrant is still in there somewhere, insisting she has managed to weather much, much worse and still survive.

2. The Extraordinary Life of the Ordinary Immigrant

It is no bad thing to celebrate a simple life.

—J.R.R. Tolkien

My father was not an important man. He toiled in restaurants his entire life, raised a family with my mother, and provided a home for us. He created, managed, and sold many businesses; the very first among them, an unpretentious little diner, Le Coin Blanc, at the corner of Henri-Julien and Mount Royal (featured on the cover of this book). He paid his taxes and routinely complained about them. He wore a Montreal Expos cap on his days off, though I don't think he had ever attended a single game and much preferred professional wrestling. He often yelled at the TV while watching the news as if he half-expected the anchor to yell back. He could be testy and had a questionable sense of humour. A gourmand, he took me out for smoked-meat sandwiches and instructed me to order them "fat or not at all." He loved a good meal and taught me to love one as well. When he retired, he took months-long vacations to Greece, puttering around in his orange or olive groves, sitting in village cafés with people who shared his childhood memories.

He loved us in that awkward, self-conscious manner of so many old-school immigrant dads. Such men didn't receive physical affection as kids and didn't know how to show it in return. He'd call to tell me to come see "how the tomato plants are doing" or "how the peach tree has grown"—code for "I miss you."

He slowed down, eventually became ill, and then, despite a stubborn desire to live, he suddenly collapsed and died one Friday afternoon in late November. I was across town, at home, getting ready to co-host a radio show later that evening when I got the call from my mother, who, unable to speak, handed the receiver over to my brother.

He was important to his family and the people around him, but no grandiose obituaries were written about him and, outside of family and close friends, no one knows where he's buried. His grandson, born after he passed away, is his namesake, but that tradition will likely end there. When my generation dies, he will be forgotten forever.

I say this without bitterness. I loved and admired my dad for what he accomplished. He mattered deeply to me and my family, but in the eyes of the world he was ordinary. The world is full of people like him who are not important enough to have articles or biographies written about them. His challenges and realities were not unlike those of so many who lived and died before him, and many who will come after him.

But he is allowed this ordinary existence and I revel in the universality of his story. As Emerson said, "I preach the infinitude of the common man."

We rejoice in the successes of extraordinary immigrants who made a significant contribution to their adopted countries. *The Washington Post* once published a piece about "immigrants who saved America and the rest of the free world."[6] Here at home, the Royal Bank of Canada hosts the annual Canadian Immigrant Awards, where inspirational stories are shared and celebrated. Canadian media emphasized the immigrant backgrounds of tennis stars Leylah Fernandez and Felix Auger-Aliassime when they shone during the US Open.[7]

While I understand the reasoning behind this, and appreciate the impulse to provide examples of the concrete benefits of welcoming people, a part of me is also annoyed.

As an immigrant, or the child of immigrants, must I save the free world to be worthy? Must I develop a new vaccine, become a sports star, save someone from a burning building, or work on the frontlines of a pandemic outbreak? Must I be exemplary in order to validate my presence?

Allow immigrants their ordinariness. Please. Let them live a life as unexciting and even mediocre as everyone else's. Let them simply raise their families, send their kids to school, pay taxes, love, and be loved. The myth of the "model minority" is too often held up as a baseline.

---

6   David N. Schwartz, "The Immigrants Who Saved America—And the Rest of The Free World," *The Washington Post*, December 2, 2017, https://www.washingtonpost.com/news/made-by-history/wp/2017/12/02/the-immigrants-who-saved-america-and-the-rest-of-the-free-world/.

7   Marcus Gee, "Canada's Young Tennis Stars Serve Up Proof of the Benefits of Immigration," *The Globe and Mail*, September 10, 2021, https://www.theglobeandmail.com/canada/toronto/article-canadas-young-tennis-stars-serve-up-proof-of-the-benefits-of/

The pressure to achieve that status, which makes all the parental sacrifices worthwhile, weighs heavily on many immigrants and their children.

In a different life, my father might have had other options. He had an enthusiasm for taking chances on business ventures my mother worried would fail, and he was often vindicated. He had an incredible memory for details, a strong work ethic, and a sharp mind. He relished life's pleasures, from the taste of a good meal to a deep belly laugh. But he was the product of his generation and a rough upbringing. Working from an early age and saddled with too many responsibilities, he had a difficult father and a far-too-meek mother. I look at pictures of him as a young soldier in Thessaloniki, riding his motorcycle, thick moustache on the upper lip of a handsome face, and I barely recognize him. Who could he have become if he were released from the constant struggle to survive?

I always thought of him as such a tough dad until my aunt, his first cousin, leaned into me after his funeral and quietly said, "Your dad was always the sweetest of the boys. He had a good heart."

How does a "good heart" get measured by an immigration points system? Who gets to quantify a person's value?

For the most part, Canada's immigration policy, first introduced in 1967, is merit-based. Applicants are assessed on their skills, adaptability, language proficiency, education, and overall "value" as newcomers. Some of these metrics are precise, for example with regards to filling specific labour market needs in certain provinces, or Quebec's understandable focus on the

French language. But in assessing cultural adaptability or language acquisition, subjectivity and bias can seep in.

Canada's system works fairly well and has succeeded in maintaining overall strong integration, retention, and satisfaction levels, as well as public trust for the process. However, government research also points out that merit and points systems can only do so much if integration systems don't also ensure that the work experience and education credentials of immigrants are recognized once they enter the country. Too often well-qualified newcomers arrive only to face discrimination, racism, limited job prospects, lack of access to language classes, or the requirement that they go back to school. The points system doesn't take any of this into account, and completely ignores the emotional reality for immigrants facing these barriers.

In addition, planning for short- and long-term labour market needs is a bit of a shot in the dark. It's hard for the slow and lumbering government bureaucracy to keep up with, let alone anticipate, ever-changing labour market needs, and the pace of change is only increasing.

I have a habit of chatting with taxi drivers, who tend to be overwhelmingly new immigrants. In all my years of speaking to them, the only one who brazenly told me he was leaving Quebec because of Bill 101—a language law that obliges children of immigrants to attend French schools—was a recently-arrived immigrant from France. He had already set in motion plans to sublet his apartment, he told me, and he and his family were weeks away from leaving for Ontario.

"I want my son to learn to speak English too," he said with passion. "I won't let the government decide that for me."

I was fascinated by this interaction, which took place in the middle of heated debates on immigration reforms by Quebec's Coalition Avenir Québec (CAQ) government in 2019.[8] As a young, educated French speaker from France, the taxi driver was a perfect example of the kind of immigrant normally welcomed in Quebec with open arms. Yet he was waving goodbye barely a year in.

Canada's immigration points system allows Quebec to prioritize French-speaking immigrants because it is assumed (rightfully, for the most part) that French speakers can more easily integrate here, and will more easily abide by language laws that prioritize French. But, as this French taxi driver had just demonstrated, a points system can't always account for people's personalities, dreams, and desires.

In sharp contrast, my Greek parents, who had the legal right to send my younger sister to English school because my brother and I had attended classes in English, did not. We decided as a family to send her to French school because it only made sense for her to do her schooling in the majority language of Quebec. She

---

8   In the fall of 2019, Quebec's CAQ government announced major reforms to its *Programme de l'expérience Québécoise* (PEQ, or Quebec Experience Program). Launched in 2010, the PEQ is a popular stream that provides a fast track to permanent residence for temporary foreign workers and international students living in Quebec. The changes were ill-conceived, and the government was forced to backtrack when faced with a major public outcry spearheaded by the workers and students who were most affected, as well as business groups who worried the reforms would limit badly-needed immigration.

is perfectly trilingual now—as are many, if not most, of Quebec's young allophones.

In April 2021, Quebec Premier François Legault was caught on tape speaking to a Quebec employers' council, saying he prefers to bring in higher-wage-earning immigrants. He was quoted as saying, "Every time the government accepts an immigrant to the province making less than $56,000, it makes it harder to achieve our goal of increasing the average salary of Quebecers."

When his speech leaked out, many were appalled at the premier's insinuation that immigrants could be reduced to their monetary value. Most second-generation immigrants know full well that their parents didn't have high-paying jobs when they first arrived. Should the door have been shut on them? What if they had been denied the right to work hard, climb the financial ladder, and build a better life? Aside from being insensitive, Legault's comments didn't even make practical sense. At the time of his speech, Quebec was facing severe labour shortages and approximately 110,000 jobs remained unfilled—jobs that paid nowhere near $56,000.

One of Legault's loudest critics was Québec Solidaire's[9] Ruba Ghazal, whose own parents had emigrated here from Lebanon. It was a long time before anyone in her family was able to earn a decent salary here.

"I worked for a long time in factories, and what I heard from him reminded me of the way we talk about products on assembly lines," Ghazal said. She had spent years working as a director of occupational health and safety in manufacturing plants before becoming a member of

9   Québec solidaire is a progressive, left-wing sovereigntist political party in Quebec.

Quebec's National Assembly (MNA). "Immigrants are not objects, let alone numbers, they are human beings."[10]

Government policies that seek only to prioritize economic-class immigration and the bottom line often miss the big picture and the long game. By focusing only on the immediate expected financial contribution, family reunification is dismissed as a lesser form of immigration that only costs and never contributes.

"If, every time we accept an economic immigrant, the federal government forces us to accept a refugee or a family reunification case, we'll have a hard time finding the right people," said Legault during that same speech.

To assume that parent sponsorship is solely a financial burden is to not understand the benefits of parents and grandparents, who often not only bring savings with them, but also emotional and social support. They help in their children's businesses and provide free childcare, allowing the parents to enter the workforce and work the crazy hours first-generation immigrants often do.

It is short-sighted to treat refugees as problems. Quebec writers Kim Thúy and Dany Laferrière were refugees. Canada's former Governor General Adrienne Clarkson was a refugee. Federal ministers Maryam Monsef and Ahmed Hussen were refugees. What people contribute to the societies that accept them cannot be measured solely by how much money we think they can make.

---

10 "Accused of Lacking Sensitivity, Quebec Premier Doubles Down on Comments about Immigrants," *The Canadian Press*, May 4, 2021, https://globalnews.ca/news/7834250/quebec-immigrants-legault-comments-backlash/.

As the daughter of a man who came to Quebec because of Canada's family reunification policy, I'm glad he was recognized as someone's brother and not treated as a number. Ordinary immigrants who quietly accomplish extraordinary things with their lives are everywhere around us.

It's time we stopped dictating immigrants' behaviour and, ultimately, their futures. Let people follow their own unique paths. Allow them their modest dreams, their ambition, their small contributions and yes, their crowning achievements. Consider them part of the whole.

In a column about her Syrian-born grandmother who later moved to Montreal, Quebec journalist Rima Elkouri writes:

Les gens s'exilent pour vivre en paix, bien sûr. Mais n'est-ce pas aussi un peu pour mourir en paix?" [11]

People go into exile to live in peace, of course. But isn't it a little bit also to die in peace?

Isn't living and dying in peace—as unexceptional as it may appear to those lucky enough to not experience abject poverty, war, government persecution, deportation, or genocide—a worthy goal in itself? Isn't that, too, extraordinary?

3. Plus ça change

From the time of early civilizations, immigrants, and refugees have been seen as dirty, untrustworthy, and lazy manipulators of the system, void of morals. To this day, nearly every immigrant demographic has fallen victim to one or more of these characterizations. It's a rite of passage.

In this country, we like to believe we are welcoming and kind to newcomers. This is the story we tell ourselves. While Canada has routinely opened its doors to immigrants, economic migrants, and refugees in need of a safer home, we haven't always made it easy for them. Of course, when we look south of the border or in other countries, we are proud of our relative openness to new immigrants. As the French saying goes, "*Quand on se compare on se console.*" When we compare ourselves, we console ourselves.

But—and oh, how that "but" can be annoying—we have an equally well-documented tradition of viewing immigrants with suspicion and fear as we treat them like parasites. We have imprisoned and exploited them and stolen from them. We have worked immigrants to death, separated them from their families, and used their cheap labour to build our national infrastructure.

We don't teach this in Canadian schools, and not knowing our collective history of systemic discrimination means we do not recognize that the suspicion and racism inflicted upon new waves of immigrants today is nothing new.

In *Racism*, sociologist Albert Memmi explores the "social pathology" of racism, referring to it as a "cultural disease" that prevails because every time we encounter a group that is different from us, we think our privileges, our property, and our security are threatened, and we employ racism as a defensive behavioural strategy.

According to Memmi, "racism has four distinct "moments:" (a) the insistence on difference, (b) the negative valuation imposed on those who are different, (c) generalizing this negative valuation to an entire group, and (d) the use of generalization to legitimize hostility."[12]

In other words, members of a majority may concede that minorities, "are not like us... they are not as good as we are... they aren't capable of fitting in here... they're all the same."

Take anyone who seems part of the socio-cultural/racial hegemony of Canada right now. If you examine their genealogy, you'll find geographic ties to Ireland, Italy, the Caribbean, Asia, or elsewhere. These very people too are the descendants of immigrants.

When the Irish arrived (the lucky ones who survived the potato famine and the coffin ships) in the eighteenth and mid-nineteenth centuries, they found only low-paying jobs in the shipyards and on the wharves. They lived in what were described as "miserable hovels which in themselves are better fitted for pig-sties and cow pens

---

12   Albert Memmi, *Racism*. (Minneapolis: University of Minnesota Press, 1999), 18.

than residences for human beings."[13] For generations, Montreal's Irish were the poorest of the poor, toiling away at factories, flour mills, and foundries, building bridges and canals, competing for jobs with equally poor French-Canadian labourers who were moving from the countryside to the city to find work. The Irish were stereotyped as uncouth, violent alcoholics, and, because of their Roman Catholic faith, were regarded as inferior by the Protestant British majority.

How did they manage to finally escape this animosity? *The Toronto Star* article quoted above attributes the shift in public perception to an important factor: language. The Irish spoke English, so sharing a common language with the majority population of Canada aided in their transition. In Quebec, many Irish immigrants assimilated into the French-speaking majority. Another important factor was that there were even newer immigrants around the corner. These arrivals, even more threatening to the majority perspective, took their place on the bottom rung. Some of those more unfamiliar immigrants were Chinese.

By the late 1880s, the most dangerous jobs, including building the Canadian Pacific Railway, were going to Chinese labourers. Earning the paltry sum of one dollar a day, they also had to pay for supplies, food, and clothing that white workers got for free. The Chinese were often assigned the responsibility for highly unpredictable explosions used to blast out sections of the mountains.[14]

---

13 Eric Andrew-Gee, "19th-Century Toronto Irish Immigrants a Lesson in Upward Mobility," *The Toronto Star*, March 14, 2015.

14 "The Legacy of Chinese Railroad Workers," *Coquitlam Heritage Blog*, July 30, 2020, https://www.coquitlamheritage.ca/blog-pages/2020/7/30/the-legacy-of-chinese-railroad-workers.

It is estimated that some four thousand Chinese workers died in the process. *A mari usque ad mare* came at a heavy price.

Once the railroad was completed, in 1885 Prime Minister John A. Macdonald introduced the first legislation to restrict immigration based on ethnicity. From that point on, the Chinese Immigration Act, as it was officially known, stipulated that every Chinese person who wanted to enter the country had to pay fifty dollars, later increased to five hundred dollars. This head tax, required only of the Chinese, was a particularly cruel deterrent to family reunification, as it made it practically impossible for men to bring over their wives and children.

The mere foreignness of immigrant groups across North America was considered a threat. The term "yellow peril" referred not to an existential threat such as war or disease, but simply because the migrants were not white. In the US, while the slur was later used to describe the growing fear of military threat from Japan, it primarily described the fear of being "invaded" by labourers from Asia.

As early as 1854, Horace Greeley, editor of the *New-York Tribune* wrote, "The Chinese are uncivilized, unclean, and filthy beyond all conception, without any of the higher domestic or social relations; lustful and sensual in their dispositions; every female is a prostitute of the basest order."[15]

Only a few years after Greeley wrote those dehumanizing sentences, ten thousand people in Vancouver

---

15 Adam Goodman, *The Deportation Machine*. (New Haven: Princeton University Press, 2020), 12.

rioted through Chinatown, terrifying residents and destroying property.

> On Sept. 7, 1907, thousands of people gathered in front of Vancouver's city hall to protest against Asian immigration to Canada. Holding signs with slogans such as 'For a White Canada,' the protestors, led by members of the newly formed Asiatic Exclusion League, stormed into the city's Chinatown neighbourhood and began rioting. Chinese-owned businesses and homes were gravely damaged, then the crowd moved onto an area of Vancouver heavily populated by Japanese immigrants. Violence ensued and the destruction continued for two days.[16]

That riot was a harbinger of things to come, one of the most famous being the anti-Greek riot of 1918 in Toronto. On August 2, 1918, thousands of disgruntled veterans gathered in Hogtown to attend a congress of the Great War Veterans' Association and voice their grievances. A Canadian army veteran who had had far too much to drink assaulted a waiter and was promptly removed from a Greek-owned café on Yonge Street. A rumour began to circulate among veterans that "one of their own" was kicked out of the café by foreigners. Greece was not yet at war with Germany, but was a friendly neutral to both the Axis and Allied powers. This prevented Greek Canadians from fighting on behalf

---

16   Barrington Walker, "Vancouver Anti-Asian Riots of 1907 and The Parallels to Canada's Modern-Day Racial Divide." Wilfrid Laurier University, November 24, 2020, https://www.wlu.ca/news/spotlights/2020/nov/vancouver-anti-asian-riots-of-1907-and-the-parallels-to-canadas-modern-day-racial-divide.html.

of Canada. Greece would eventually enter the war, but the false narrative of these immigrant men "not doing their part" contributed to the community's vilification. The simmering resentment was a tinderbox waiting for a spark.

The incident would end up triggering the biggest race riot the city has ever known, and one of the largest anti-Greek riots in the world. "By the time it was all over—after then-mayor Tommy Church invoked the Riot Act and called in the military police—hundreds would be injured, many would be arrested, and damage to Greek property would total more than $1 million by today's values."[17] As quoted by historian Thomas Gallant in the documentary *Violent August*, "Tonight, they would go hunting Greeks."[18] Every Greek-owned business was destroyed as Toronto police did nothing.

The treatment of Toronto's Greek community was representative of attitudes throughout North America. In 1909, a pogrom-style riot in Nebraska resulted in the death of a young Greek boy and the burning of Greek-owned businesses and homes. South Omaha's Greek community was forced to leave for its own safety. Greek immigrants in the US, like many other new minorities at the time, were viewed with suspicion, looked down upon as inferior, and generally seen as job stealers.

"Herded together in lodging houses and living cheaply, Greeks are a menace to the American labouring man—just as the Japs, Italians, and other similar

---

17   Toula Drimonis, "A Century Later, a Vicious Anti-Greek Riot in Toronto Offers Lessons for Today," *Maclean's*, August 1, 2018.

18   *Violent August: The 1918 Anti-Greek Riots in Toronto*, directed by John Burry (2009: Burgeoning Communications Inc., 2009), DVD.

labourers are," Joseph Pulcar, the editor of the *Omaha Daily News*, wrote at the time.[19]

Greeks were even targets of the Ku Klux Klan (KKK). The American Hellenic Educational Progressive Association (AHEPA)—one of the largest Hellenic heritage groups in the world—was founded in 1922 in direct response to the racism and bigotry Greeks experienced at the hands of the KKK. While it's barely remembered today, the Greek population was, in fact, terrorized by the racist organization who saw all immigrants and people of colour as lesser than. Greeks were depicted by the organization as prone to criminality, being "unassimilated, unfit, unAmericanized and unsafe aliens" that contributed three times their share to "Our Alien Crime Plague."[20]

The KKK organized boycotts of Greek-owned confectionaries and restaurants, and amplified its tactics by openly threatening or attacking customers. "Greek establishments doing as much as $500 to $1,000 a day business, especially in the South and Midwest, dropped to as little as $25 a day," James S. Scofield wrote in a 1997 article for AHEPA. "The only recourse was to sell or close."[21]

The KKK was an equal-opportunity hater, and French Canadians who had moved to Maine in the 1920s to work in the mills were not exempt. Like other targeted groups, the KKK worried they would unionize,

---

19   Gerontakis Steven, "AHEPA vs. the KKK Greek-Americans on the Path to Whiteness," University of North Carolina, http://toto.lib.unca.edu/sr_papers/history_sr/srhistory_2012/gerontakis_steven.pdf.

20   H.W. Evans, "Our Alien Crime Plague and its Cure," *The Kourier Magazine*, March 1926, 1-4.

21   Drimonis, "A Vicious Anti-Greek Riot in Toronto."

demanding better wages and working conditions.[22] Their arguments consisted of the routine xenophobic tropes of immigrants "stealing our jobs and depressing our wages."

At the turn of the twentieth century, when close to one million French Canadians moved to the US for a better future, some permanently and some as temporary workers, they were described as "half-wild" and "primitive." Like the Italians, the Greeks, and the Jews, Quebec loggers were seen as "between white and non-white."[23] Proximity to the new country and race did not shield them from discrimination. As long as they were poor and foreign, they were suspect. This treatment, of course, wasn't only doled out by individuals. Governments legalized popular racist sentiments, and Canada was no better than others at the time.

The twentieth century is full of blatant examples of Canadian anti-immigrant legislation. In 1908, for example, the Continuous Passage Act stipulated that only those immigrants who had travelled directly from their home country to Canada, with no stops, were accepted. The legislation was meant to keep out non-European nationals, such as migrants from Japan and India, as there were no direct steamship routes to Canada from those countries at the time. Even if someone from India, for example, managed to bypass these restrictions, they needed to pay two hundred dollars (eight times the amount required of white immigrants) just to disembark. The end game was obvious: to slow or shut down

---

22 Jean-François Nadeau, "Quand le KKK faisait sa loi contre les Canadiens-français du Maine," *Le Devoir*, June 8, 2021.

23 Sarah R. Champagne, "Les Canadiens-français, ces migrants 'pas tout à fait blancs,'" *Le Devoir*, October 20, 2021.

the flow of Indian immigrants coming to Canada in search of work. This discriminatory and exclusionary condition would not come to an end until 1967.

The Immigration Act, first passed in 1906 and updated in 1910, stated that the government had the authority to block "immigrants belonging to any race deemed unsuited to the climate or requirements of Canada," an arbitrary and undefined rule that enabled unfettered discrimination. Prospective immigrants were listed in order of desirability, with white American and British immigrants at the top of the list. At the bottom were Jews, Asians, Roma, and pretty much anyone with dark skin.

Most people don't know that Canada could have had a Caribbean island as a province in the early 1900s, were it not for racism. The islands of choice at the time were Jamaica, then Bermuda, and later the Bahamas. "There was a movement and a promotional campaign," says history professor Sarah-Jane (Saje) Mathieu, author of *North of the Colour Line: Migration and Black Resistance in Canada, 1870-1955*, on the CBC podcast, *Secret Life of Canada*.[24]

"The problem was the Black folks in the Caribbean and to what extent their incorporation would rattle Canadian democracy," she explains. "In effect, we decided that it would be too frightening an enterprise."

Podcast co-hosts Leah-Simone Bowen and Falen Johnson conclude that Canada found the Caribbean an attractive option for a dual citizenship vacation, work,

---

24   Sarah-Jane (Sage) Mathieu, "The Province of Jamaica," Secret Life of Canada (podcast), Season 2, Episode 11, CBC, February 19, 2019.

or trade destination, but didn't necessarily want to open the door wide open to Black migration to Canada.

In 1911, there was a failed attempt to make the Bahamas part of Canada. The Bahamian colonial legislature, backed by prominent Canadian investors, pushed hard to join. The Royal Bank of Canada had established an office in Nassau in 1908 and there was money to be made investing in infrastructure. Even Prime Minister Wilfred Laurier was open to the idea.

According to George Washington University's Noel Maurer, at around the same time a group of about a thousand wealthy Black Americans fleeing Jim Crow laws arrived at the Canadian border, resulting in panic.[25] Many Canadians, especially those in the newly established province of Alberta, wrote to their political representatives expressing fears that "Negro immigration" would force the white folks to leave the Prairies, drive property values down, and make "their women" unsafe. It wasn't the time to be selling Canadians on the idea of a Black-populated province.

While the Canadian government wasn't blocking Black immigration from the US outright, it did everything it could to dissuade Black immigrants. The government even hired a Black doctor to travel to Oklahoma and lecture about the terrible Canadian climate. Finally, with a federal election looming, the decision was made to use the aforementioned Immigration Act of 1910, which, as I stated earlier, allowed the government to ban

---

25   Noel Maurer, "Fear of a Black Canada," *The Power and the Money*, August 10, 2011, https://noelmaurer.typepad.com/aab/2011/08/disgraceful-canadian-initiative.html.

"immigrants belonging to any race deemed unsuited to the climate or requirements of Canada."

Arbitrary reasons like climate suitability were simply a way of justifying the fact that Canada was opening the door to many European immigrants at the time, while shutting out Black and Brown people from the British Commonwealth. Because, if we're being honest, *few* Canadians are suited to the climate of this country!

When Laurier lost the next election, the Bahamians tried again. Island governor William Grey-Wilson travelled to Canada to jumpstart the conversation, but Prime Minister Robert Borden was convinced that most Canadians would not accept a majority-Black province, no matter how small or how far away.

The overall idea eventually fell through, explains Maurer, because resistance didn't come only from Canadians, but also from the British Crown, which was not keen on losing its lucrative Caribbean territories to its Canadian colony. "What we don't realize is that we got Newfoundland instead of Jamaica as a concession from England,"[26] explains Mathieu.

In 1914, a major event in Canadian immigration history took place when the Komagata Maru, a ship carrying 376 Sikh, Muslim, and Hindu Punjabi immigrants from British India, arrived at Canadian shores but was not allowed to dock. Newspapers of the day warned of the "Hindu invasion."[27] Passengers were forcibly kept on the boat for two long months with no water or food

26 Mathieu, "The Province of Jamaica."
27 Voyage of the "Undesirables: Remembering the Komagata Maru," CBC Radio One, Ideas documentary series, episode first aired May 23, 2014, https://www.cbc.ca/radio/ideas/voyage-of-the-undesirables-remembering-the-komagata-maru-1.2914096

supplied, making do with what they had on the ship. Even though some argued that Komagata Maru passengers were British subjects and should have been allowed to move to another country in the British Empire, they were denied entry.

Sir Richard McBride, the Conservative premier of British Columbia, made it very clear what the official government goal was at the time. "To admit Orientals in large numbers would mean the end, the extinction of the white people," he said. "We always have in mind the necessity of keeping this a white man's country."[28] When the passengers were turned away and returned to India, many were imprisoned or killed by the British.

In 2016, Canada issued an official apology to the descendants of the people on that ship. "As a nation, we should never forget the prejudice suffered by the Sikh community at the hands of the Canadian government of the day," said Prime Minister Justin Trudeau. "Who would think that 102 years later, when the apology finally came in Parliament, that Canada would have four Sikh ministers, including the Minister of Defence who at one time was the first Sikh person to lead a regiment in Canada? And that it would be the very same regiment that turned passengers at the Komagata Maru away?"[29]

Overt racism subsides, but bias always lives below the surface. Over a hundred years after the last Chinese immigrant worked the railroad, Asians are considered examples of successful immigration for their

---

28   Matt Ford, "Canada's Long-Awaited Apology," *The Atlantic*, May 18, 2016.

29   Matthew McRae, "The Story of the Komagata Maru," Canadian Museum for Human Rights, March 22, 2022, https://humanrights.ca/story/the-story-of-the-komagata-maru.

extraordinary socioeconomic achievements while still often being seen as perpetual foreigners. Despite incredible efforts on the part of new Canadians to be accepted into the majority, their conditional status often remains. All it takes is a single event that shakes up a hard-earned, delicate balance to remind them of that.

In early 2020, when COVID-19 began inflicting its deadly damage, many were quick to point the finger at China and the Chinese—not over legitimate concerns about the Chinese government's secrecy and Beijing's initial attempts to keep the virus' deadly toll under wraps. Rather, Asians in general were being held responsible for the very virus itself. The incessant ranting about the "China virus" was quickly adopted by bigots. Almost immediately, the focus became the Chinese community's eating habits (as if the rest of the world's factory-farmed meat wasn't responsible for bird flu and swine flu). Bats and wet markets were suddenly the topics of many uninformed conversations. Clear xenophobia ran through everything, with racist memes that called Asians "barbaric" spreading just as quickly as the virus.

Early on in the pandemic, individuals of Asian descent across North America and Europe became the targets of random racist attacks. Buddhist temples in Montreal were vandalized.[30] Vietnamese and Korean businesses incurred damages. Hateful graffiti appeared in Montreal's Chinatown. A ninety-two-year-old Asian man with dementia was assaulted in a racially motivated attack in East Vancouver by a white man in his fifties. As

---

30   Morgan Lowrie, "Montreal Police Investigating Recent Vandalism at Buddhist Temples as Potential Hate Crimes," *The Globe and Mail*, March 4, 2020.

with the SARS outbreak in 2003, Asians were bullied, attacked, or accosted on the street simply because they were Asian.[31]

It got so bad that on April 16, 2020, the Montreal-based Centre for Research-Action on Race Relations (CRARR) joined forces with about a dozen community organizations to issue a call for the federal government to take concrete actions to combat rising anti-Asian racism and hate linked to COVID-19. They launched a bilingual campaign with the message, "COVID-19 does not discriminate. Neither should you."[32]

In March of 2021, a government-funded report, *A Year of Racist Attacks: Anti-Asian Racism Across Canada One Year into the COVID-19 Pandemic*,[33] was released by the Toronto chapter of the Chinese Canadian National Council. It revealed that more than 1,100 incidents of anti-Asian attacks had taken place in the first year of the pandemic, with 73 percent involving verbal harassment, 11 percent physical assault or unwanted physical contact, and 10 percent being coughed or spat on. The very young or the very old were most targeted. A total of 40 percent of all incidents occurred in Ontario, while 44 percent took place in British Columbia. Vancouver police confirmed that anti-Asian attacks had increased

---

31 Kamila Hinkson, "Montreal's Korean Consulate Issues Safety Warning After Man Stabbed," CBC News, March 18, 2020.

32 CRARR launches campaign against Covid-19-related discrimination, Centre for Research- Action on Race Relations, April 1, 2020. CRARR website press release, April 1, 2020. http://www.crarr.org/?q=node/20092

33 Jeremiah Rodriguez, "New Report Details 'Disturbing Rise' in Anti-Asian Hate Crimes in Canada," CTV News, March 23, 2021.

by a whopping 717 percent over the last year, from 12 to 142 cases.[34]

History has shown us that when destabilizing events, such as a deadly global pandemic, threaten people's overall sense of individual or communal safety, they also serve to remind immigrants or their descendants that they remain "foreign."

"The assumption," writes Asian-American actor John Cho, who immigrated to the US at the age of six, "was that once we became American enough we would be safe... The hope was that race would not disadvantage us—the next generation—if we played our cards right." Cho talks about leading a life "devoid of race" and experiencing the illusion of "raceless-ness," but suddenly realizing during the pandemic that "our belonging is conditional. One minute we are Americans, the next we are all foreigners, who 'brought' the virus here."[35]

That conditional status is one that most immigrants or their children can relate to. They know it when their name, their religion, their accent, their mother tongue, their political loyalties or personal affinities are questioned in moments of crisis or national uncertainty. Internment camps are the perfect historical manifestation of the conditional status of immigrants, with Canada's Italian and Japanese communities suffering the brunt of it in this country's not-so-distant past.

---

34 Terry Haig, "New Report Finds Anti-Asian Racist Incidents on the Rise in Canada," Radio-Canada International, March 24, 2021.

35 John Cho, "Coronavirus Reminds Asian Americans Like Me That Our Belonging is Conditional," *Los Angeles Times*, April 22, 2020, https://www.latimes.com/opinion/story/2020-04-22/asian-american-discrimination-john-cho-coronavirus.

Canada's Italian community may be an integral part of the country at present, but it wasn't always the case. When Italians first began arriving in North America in the early nineteenth century, they were classified as "non-preferred" and seen as "hordes of dark, dirty, ignorant, lazy, subversive, superstitious criminals" who were "prone to violence."[36] Italian immigrants to Canada in the early twentieth century and after World War II were poor, unskilled, and willing to work anywhere. They were necessary to Canada's rapidly growing economy, but still regarded with animosity.

"In a 1949 government memo, Canada's commissioner for overseas immigration, Laval Fortier, wrote that the Italian 'peasant' is 'not the type of immigrant we are looking for in Canada. His standard of living, his way of life, even his civilization seems so different that I doubt if he could ever become an asset to our country.'"[37]

War only amplified this suspicion. In 1940, more than 30,000 Italian Canadians were classified as "enemy aliens" and more than 600 forced into internment camps, suspected of being fascists and disloyal to the state. Using the War Measures Act, Prime Minister William Mackenzie King gave the government power to revoke the rights and seize the property of anyone suspected of being an enemy alien. There was no trial or proof, and no Italian Canadians were ever charged with criminal activity or being a "subversive element."

---

36 Davide Mastracci, "Let Them Eat Cake," *Maisonneuve*, January 12, 2017, https://maisonneuve.org/article/2017/01/12/let-them-eat-cake/.

37 Davide Mastracci, "As a Proud Italian-Canadian, I Won't Stand by My Community's Racism," *Huffington Post Canada*, July 14, 2018, https://www.huffingtonpost.ca/davide-mastracci/italian-canadian-immigrant-racism-mangiacake_a_23476352/.

"Thousands of Italian Canadians were declared illegal aliens, families were destroyed, lives were destroyed," Federal Justice Minister David Lametti (himself of Italian origin) was quoted as saying in 2019, after Prime Minister Justin Trudeau committed to making an apology to Italian Canadians interned during World War II. He finally did in May of 2021.[38]

Italian Canadian Vittorio Rossi's play *Paradise by the River* recounts the plight of those who were arrested and placed in Camp Petawawa (also known as Camp 33) in Ontario during World War II. It tells the story of Romano Dicenzo, arrested without charges in his home in Montreal and sent away from his pregnant wife Maria. He remains there as a prisoner of war for four years while his family is left to survive on a stipend of $12 per month. The play is an important piece of history-based storytelling.

The Japanese community fared even worse. After the attack at Pearl Harbor in 1941, the Royal Canadian Mounted Police rounded up Japanese Canadians. Men between the ages of 18 and 45 were sent away to hard labour, while men over 45 and women and children were sent to internment camps. Families were separated, and the government seized their property, including farms and businesses. Many members of the Japanese community had owned lucrative fishing boats on the British Columbia coast. Ottawa seized it all, initially renting them out and promising the internees that everything would be returned after the war. But, not even a year

---

38   Christine Long and Selena Ross, "Italian-Canadians Waiting for Delayed Apology Over Internment Camps," CTV News, June 10, 2020, https://montreal.ctvnews.ca/italian-canadians-waiting-for-delayed-apology-over-internment-camps-1.4979291.

later, the government reversed its decision and sold everything off hoping to deter Japanese Canadians from returning to the BC coast. After the war, the government was pressured to offer some compensation to owners, but at prices far below market value. To add insult to injury, the interned Japanese were forced to pay for their stay in the camps.

More than 20,000 Japanese Canadians were thrown into camps, among them the well-known Canadian-born geneticist and environmental activist David Suzuki, whose parents were Canadian-born as well. Suzuki, now a source of national pride, spent three years in an internment camp in Slocan, BC. His youngest sister was born there. Like so many others, they had to give up most of what they owned and were forced to resettle in Ontario.

When the war was over, Japanese Canadians were banned from returning to BC and never compensated for their property—much of which had been given away or sold at bargain-basement prices—despite the fact that not a single person was ever charged with espionage. They were told to settle east of the Rockies or be deported to Japan, a country most of them had never seen. Approximately 4,000, most of them older, first-generation immigrants, chose to leave for bombed-out Japan. It wouldn't be until 1949 that Japanese Canadians would be allowed to reside within 160 kilometres of the coast of British Columbia. In 1988, Canada apologized to the Japanese community and offered compensation to those who had been interned.

Today, people like to think that they would have been one of the good guys, if they had been around during the Holocaust. But in 1939 the world already knew

Jews were being persecuted in Germany. Kristallnacht, a pogrom carried out by the Nazis that included the burning of hundreds of synagogues, the destroying of businesses, and the arrest of thousands of Jewish men in 1938, was still fresh in people's minds. German prison camps, which would soon become death camps, were materializing. If a ship filled with desperate, stateless, Jewish refugees from Germany docked on Canadian shores, the country would rush to take them in, right?

Wrong.

On June 7, 1939, the MS St. Louis, carrying more than 900 refugees fleeing Nazi Germany, arrived in Halifax. The ship had already attempted to dock in Cuba and the US and had been turned away. But when the ship sought permission to disembark its occupants, Frederick Blair, Deputy Minister of Immigration, expressed concerns over allowing Jewish refugees to seek sanctuary here. "The line must be drawn somewhere," he said.

And so, the line was drawn. Unable to dock anywhere, the ship returned its passengers to Belgium where they dispersed to different European countries, hoping to survive. Many of them did not; 254 of the passengers, many of them children, perished in the Holocaust.

Between 1933 and 1945, Canada admitted fewer than five thousand Jewish refugees—the lowest number among developed nations. To understand how low that number is, Britain admitted seventy thousand during that same time period. Anti-Semitism dictated much of our immigration policy at the time. When Blair was asked how many Jews should be admitted to Canada at the end of the Second World War, he famously replied,

"None is too many."[39] The statement was not controversial at the time.

Since then, thankfully, much has evolved with regard to our immigration policies, and Canada has been recognized as a leader in helping those less fortunate. In the past fifty years, more than half a million refugees have been resettled in Canada, close to half of them via the direct support of Canadians through the Private Sponsorship of Refugees Program, which was launched in 1979.

In the 1960s, Haitians began arriving in Canada, fleeing the dictatorship of François Duvalier, known as Papa Doc. Due to their fluency in French, they primarily settled in Quebec. "Haitian immigration increased exponentially in the early 1970s. In 1973 and 1974, Haitians ranked first among all of the migratory groups who came to Quebec."[40] Thanks to their strong ties to francophone culture and the Roman Catholic church, they were, for the most part, well received and have become an integral part of Quebec society.

Between 1979 and 1980, more than 60,000 Southeast-Asian (Vietnamese and Cambodian) refugees came to Canada, many of them also settling in French-speaking Quebec. The Parti Québécois (PQ) government at the time was quite willing to welcome those in need. Immigration Minister Jacques Couture, who sought to speed up the refugee selection process, was quoted as saying, "We won't save the Cambodian people, or the

---

39 Eli Yarhi, "MS St. Louis," *The Canadian Encyclopedia*, May 27, 2019, https://www.thecanadianencyclopedia.ca/en/article/ms-st-louis

40 Alain Saint-Victor, "Haitian Canadians," *The Canadian Encyclopedia*, August 5, 2021, https://www.thecanadianencyclopedia.ca/en/article/haitian-canadians.

Khmer civilization, but we can save human lives, maybe a few thousand perhaps?"[41] How refreshing to see an immigration minister open to… immigration.

"About 7,000 Vietnamese came to Canada in the five months after the fall of Saigon," writes Tu Thanh Ha in *The Globe and Mail*.[42] "After we landed in Montreal, with $350 as our entire net worth, my parents started anew. Their professional credentials weren't recognized, so my mother, a pharmacist in her 30s, worked as a parking-lot attendant and then as a clerk in a clothing store."

Not unlike Syrian refugees in recent years, most Southeast-Asian refugees were sponsored by community groups, churches, and private individuals. These "boat people" have since been successfully absorbed into the fold and, just like all immigrants before them, their descendants continue to contribute to their home.

In 1986, Canada was awarded the UNHCR Nansen Refugee Award, the first time it was ever given to an entire country instead of an individual or an organization. The award honoured those who "go above and beyond the call of duty to protect refugees, displaced and stateless people."

In 2015, the Syrian refugee crisis was making headlines. Encouraged by the public outrage caused by the heartbreaking image of young Syrian refugee boy Alan Kurdi's lifeless body on a beach, Justin Trudeau's Liberals promised both to resettle the refugees if elected and to make progressive immigration policy changes.

---

41   Madeleine Berthault, "Couture facilite l'entrée des réfugiés au Québec," *La Presse*, July 21, 1979.

42   Tu Thanh Ha, "A Chance at a New Life After the Fall of Saigon 40 Years Ago," *The Globe and Mail*, April 24, 2015.

By 2019, the Liberal government had resettled almost 60,000 Syrians. That's no small feat, and despite my many issues with Trudeau's administration, this gesture is one I will always commend. Despite ongoing backlogs and bureaucratic delays, these recent policies have cemented Canada's new position as a country that leads by example. "Thank God for Canada!" read a 2019 *New York Times* headline.

Despite our increasing willingness to welcome new waves of immigration, anti-immigrant sentiment persists. In the fall of 2021, Ontario Premier Doug Ford stated that he was looking for "hard-working" immigrants to help fill the labour gap. "You come here like every other new Canadian, you work your tail off. If you think you're coming to collect the dole and sit around, not going to happen. Go somewhere else."[43]

Ford's derogatory comments, playing on popular racist tropes of the lazy immigrant who moves here to milk the system, sparked outrage among voters, particularly first- and second-generation Canadians. It was a direct attack on their families, who had toiled to build a life here.

The implication of his comments was also patently false. Not only are most permanent newcomers to Canada skilled workers, who are on average better-educated than Canadian-born workers and who must show proof of employment, reliable income, financial security, or family sponsorship to be accepted, they're

---

43 Abby Newfeld, "Doug Ford Asked to Apologize Over 'Divisive' Comments About Immigrants," CTV News, October 18, 2021.

also rarely a drain on the system.[44] What's more, *their* children become more educated and higher paid than the Canadian average.[45] Yes, there may be an initial and often temporary fiscal burden incurred by Canada when receiving newcomers, but considering the significant barriers credentialed immigrants face in finding work to match their skill levels, his comments were insulting. How many doctors, professors, and engineers are driving cabs, working the cash at Costco, caring for seniors in long-term care centres or working in warehouses because their foreign credentials aren't accepted? How many Uber shifts do these new immigrants tackle while often also learning a new language and working menial jobs, hoping the future will be better for their children? Finally, how many new immigrants lost their lives to COVID because of the dangerous working conditions at their low-paid jobs?

And yet, although the facts did not support the premier's comments, he went there. Because the tropes of the bad immigrant persist, and because many Canadians continue to buy into them. In Quebec, pundits push the idea of immigrants "diluting" our values, and some columnists have referred to immigration as the "demographic drowning of Quebec's francophone population."[46]

Despite the well-documented history of the many contributions immigrants have made to Canada's

44   Colin R. Singer, "Immigrants More Educated than Canadians," *The National Post*, January 24, 2019.

45   Shelby Thevenot, "Immigrant Children Become More Educated and Higher Paid than Canadian Average: Study," CIC News, February 8, 2022.

46   Mathieu Bock-Côté, "La noyade démographique du peuple québécois," *Le Journal de Montréal*, April 7, 2021.

economic vitality, some continue to believe these harmful clichés. We continue to look on these new "others" with mistrust, wondering if they will share "our" values and "our" way of life.

History has shown us that they do.

4. Say My Name

These white people can pronounce wild shit like
Worcestershire and Buttigieg, but as soon as an
ethnic name comes around they stutter.

—Twitter

My father's name was Panayote, a common Greek name. Meaning "all holy," it derives from the Greek term Panagia or Panayia for Mary, mother of Jesus. The feminine form is Panayiota.

My father became Peter when he moved to Canada. He joined fellow Greeks like Yiannis who became John, Constantinos who became Gus, Vasilios who became Billy, and so on and so forth. Immigrants with little education, non-existent English, and in quick need of a name that Canadians could easily pronounce, picked whatever sounded about right. If it was phonetically close, it passed muster.

My mother's name is Ourania. That was her paternal grandmother's name, but it's also much more than just another saint's name. Ourania is one of the nine muses of Greek mythology. Her name means "heavenly" or "of the heavens." She was the muse of astronomy, and *ouranos* in modern Greek means sky. Absolutely no one referred to my mom as Ourania in Canada; she shortened it to Rena. My niece, who has my mother's name, goes by Nia.

My full name is Archontoula, my paternal grandmother's name. It is derived from Archontia, from the ancient Greek word, *arche*, which means "beginning" or "first place," denoting authority over others, or *nobility*. Modern English words like architecture, archnemesis, and archbishop are derived from the root of my name. Except for my grandmothers, who used to call me by my given name, no one calls me that anymore. I introduce myself as Toula.

As a kid, I used to think my given name was hopelessly pretentious, but as an adult I appreciate how unusual it is. In my entire life I have only come across a single Archontoula I wasn't related to. Occasionally, a poor sucker of a telemarketer has my full legal name on their list, and I listen to them struggle to pronounce the guttural "ch" as it sticks in their throat. I let them try. It's a small price I feel they should have to pay for bothering me while I'm trying to work or eat. They never, ever succeed.

As someone with a non-mainstream "exotic" name (that's what I'm told by non-Greeks), I'm always shocked that people mispronounce and misspell even its derivative, *Toula*, such a simple two-syllable word.

A former politician and current broadcaster recently emailed to thank me for writing a feisty column criticizing the provincial government. It was a good column and I was pleased that he had taken the time to email me about it. But he kept referring to me as Ms. Toulis, which on hindsight I suspect was a mashup of my first and last names. I thought, "It's right there in the byline. I realize you may have not encountered my name before, but could you have not taken an extra second to verify its spelling before pressing send?" And this isn't an isolated incident. I worked with people in print media who have routinely botched my name for over a decade.

A person's given name is sacred. It matters because it's the name given to them by their parents. In many cases, it has been passed down for generations. Traditionally, Greeks pass down the father's parents' names. Boys are named after the paternal grandfather and girls after the paternal grandmother. If there's a third child, the maternal grandparents might get a chance to have namesakes. It was once considered an insult to not name your children after your parents, and privileging the names of the paternal grandparents is, of course, patriarchy at work, but the tradition is no longer as sacrosanct as it once was. Nowadays, Greek parents won't cause a family rift if they call their kids something else.

Regardless of how you got your name, it's an integral part of who you are and where you come from. But, often, if you're an allophone, an immigrant, or the child of one, it also signals your otherness.

Saying a person's name accurately—or at the very least, making the attempt—is a sign of respect. It's not trivial to get it wrong all the time, or to substitute it with an easier-to-you nickname. Yes, "ethnic" names may be difficult to pronounce to the ear used to Jacks and Jills, but it's careless and rude to not even try.

When Hockey Canada told the French speaking announcer at the 2018 Pyeongchang Olympics to pronounce the names of three francophone hockey players the English way, Quebec's French-language media and politicians lost it. Philippe Couillard, then Quebec premier, called the directive "deplorable" and PQ MNA Pascal Bérubé said it was insulting and showed a lack of respect. Federal Heritage Minister Mélanie Joly promised to follow up to ensure that Hockey Canada changed its policy.[47]

After the dust had settled, and questions had been asked, it turned out that there was, in fact, no official Hockey Canada policy. The request had been made by the players themselves, who all pronounce their names in the English way.

As heated as the overreaction was, it illustrates not only how sensitive the issue of language is in Quebec, but also how often French names are mispronounced in the rest of the country—a country that is officially bilingual. Don Cherry used to routinely botch Patrick Roy's name. (In his defence, he used to botch the names of players from all ethnic backgrounds.) Brian Lilley, a TV personality working for the now-defunct Sun News Network (ironically owned at the time by French-language media conglomerate Quebecor) made headlines when he scoffed at the efforts CBC anchors made to properly pronounce French names.

"If you listen to CBC, you wouldn't even know that Charles Ham-a-lin had won a gold because he's *Sharle Am-e-leh, oui*," he said. "Broadcasters in this country think that they have to go all native and speak a foreign language just because they're pronouncing somebody's name."[48]

---

47   Lynn Desjardins, "Outrage in Canada Over Pronunciation of Names at Olympics," *Radio-Canada International*, February 27, 2018.

48   Amanda Kelly, "Pronunciation Matters: How Should Canadian Athletes' Names be Pronounced?" *Global News*, February 11, 2014.

"A foreign language."

Is it any wonder francophones in Quebec and across the country feel slighted at the lack of effort made to honour and pronounce their names properly? It might seem like a minor inconvenience to those with mainstream names, but I can assure you it isn't:

> Research has observed that the mispronunciation of names for racialized people can lead to anxiety and resentment towards their names; in other words, this constant micro-aggression can foster internalized racism. Kohli and Solorzano (2012) refer to it as a form of cultural disrespect that confirms difference and otherness. Cultural disrespect can also be applied to French Canadians living/working in the very Anglophile countries of Canada and/or America. To dismiss the importance of pronouncing someone's name correctly (or the need for a reasonable effort) is also to dismiss the value of the person.[49]

The disrespect can go both ways. I've seen more than a few francophone Quebecers purposefully refer to former Quebec Premier Jean Charest as John James Charest when attempting to insult him or to imply that he's not a real Quebecer. There's a certain irony in watching a linguistic minority preoccupied with maintaining their heritage—which includes their French names—vilify and mock English names that are historically just as Québécois as theirs.[50] The message unfortunately

49 Courtney Szto, "What's in a Name? A Lot, Actually," *Hockey in Society*, October 20, 2019, https://hockeyinsociety.com/2019/10/20/whats-in-a-name-a-lot-actually.
50 Nathalie Tremblay, "John James ou Jean Charest," *Le Soleil,* September 14, 2010.

communicated to the many of us who don't have French first and last names is that we aren't real Quebecers.

Orange Is the New Black actress Uzo Aduba was once asked if she ever considered changing her name. Aduba, whose full name is Uzoamaka (which means "the road is good" in Igbo), asked her mom when she was young to change it to Zoe. But her mother replied, "If they can learn to say Tchaikovsky and Michelangelo and Dostoyevsky, they can learn to say Uzoamaka."[51]

Journalist Raisa Patel wrote a CBC opinion piece in 2019 explaining how she came to the realization that her name deserved respect, too. "It may seem trivial to complain about the way your name is pronounced, which is why I don't correct every offender. When you're a woman of colour who has learned to be grateful for her place in the world, the last thing you want to do is challenge a person of authority about something as simple as a name... As a child, I never dared to correct my teachers and went by names unrecognizable from my own, sometimes for years."[52]

Most "ethnic" families will debate how they name their children, taking into consideration white Western society and the dominant culture. They worry about whether people will know how to spell or pronounce these supposedly "difficult" names. They worry about bureaucracy, red tape, and confusion from Revenu Québec or school teachers. They worry whether someone with a different name will be subjected to prejudice, or whether

---

51 Jessica Dickerson, "Why Uzo Aduba Wouldn't Change Her Nigerian Name For Acting," *Huffington Post*, June 26, 2014.

52 Raisa Patel, "Here's How to Pronounce My Name, and Why it Matters to Me," *CBC News*, January 3, 2019, https://www.cbc.ca/news/canada/ottawa/pov-raisa-different-name-1.4952640.

their children will resent being saddled with names that are forever mangled and misspelled. They're not wrong to be worried.

A 2012 situation test carried out by the Quebec Human Rights Commission found that corporate recruiters given resumés identical in everything but name were 72 percent more likely to respond to "white" names (names common among English- and French-speaking Quebecers) over those that sounded African, Arabic, or Hispanic.[53] The same commission found that "in 2015, racialized people had an unemployment rate of two to three times that of non-racialized people." The situation persisted across all levels of education.

This reality, which exists across Canada, leads some people to "whiten" their CVs. Prestigious degrees and years of relevant experience may often mean very little when a foreign-sounding name prevents them from even getting an interview, let alone a call back.

For a 2012 University of Toronto study titled "Why Do Some Employers Prefer to Interview Matthew, but Not Samir?" researchers Philip Oreopoulos and Diane Dechief sent CVs to employers in Toronto, Montreal, and Vancouver. They found applicants with Chinese, Indian, Greek, or Pakistani names were 40 percent less likely to get an interview than those with Western European names.[54] Canada is not unique in its hesitation regarding

53   Toula Drimonis, "Quebec is Reviewing Systemic Racism. Canada Should Follow," *National Observer*, August 15, 2017.

54   Philip Oreopoulos and Diane DeChief, "Why Do Some Employers Prefer to Interview Matthew, but Not Samir? New evidence from Toronto, Montreal, and Vancouver," *SSRN*, February 2012, https://bit.ly/3FKXiIg.

ethnic-sounding names. Similar studies in the US, UK, Australia, and France revealed the same thing.

Name-based bias is faced both by immigrants and their descendants. A good friend of mine, an Algerian Quebecer, once told me that to offset any potential bias about his Muslim name, he's made sure to emphasize his graduation from the prestigious private Collège Brébeuf on his curriculum vitae.

In Quebec, a man called Mostafa Benomar tried to legally change his name because he felt it was the cause of discrimination against him.[55] Not finding this a valid reason, the provincial government refused. Benomar maintained that his Muslim-sounding name has cost him job opportunities.

A name's likeability, popularity, familiarity, and appeal to employers is, of course, subjective and always depends on the majority group. "Strange" allophone names stick out like a sore thumb. A foreign name may brand people as not Canadian enough, not Québécois enough, forever from "somewhere else."

A tweet by Toronto lawyer Hadiya Roderique lamenting the double standards and sheer subjectivity of what names are considered strange made me laugh: "Today, someone told me that my name, which is Swahili/Arabic and means gift or guide to righteousness, was 'weird'. Funny coming from a guy named John whose name also means toilet."

As Toronto author and educator Shakil Choudhury says in his book *Deep Diversity*, "the power to define

---

55   Trudie Mason, "Montreal Man Suing to Get Muslim-Sounding Name Changed," *CJAD*, January 8, 2019.

normal is one of the systemic powers generally invisible to dominant groups."[56]

My sister made a calculated decision to give her son our father's name to honour our family legacy and a dad she loved. She and her husband had a secret pact none of us knew about until after she gave birth. If the child were a boy, they would name him after my dad, who passed away in 2013. If a girl, she would be named after her husband's mom, whom he lost to cancer at the tender age of eleven.

And, so, they named him Panayote. Not Peter, not Pete, but Panayote. It's a bold decision to name a child something that isn't easy to pronounce and that brands him as not part of the Roman Catholic majority. It's also a concession my Italian brother-in-law made out of love. I admire and appreciate him for it.

In a way, it's coming full circle when a second-generation immigrant daughter chooses to honour her dad by giving her son his actual name rather than the anglicized version. "Peter" would have been the easy way out. It says a lot about her faith in a multicultural Canada that she had no qualms about giving her son the foreign-sounding name that had been given to his grandfather in a tiny

Greek village decades ago and an ocean away.

---

56   Shakil Choudhury, *Deep Diversity: Overcoming Us Vs. Them*. (Toronto: Between the Lines, 2015), 40.

5. Where Are You From?

Nothing has the power to divide people as much as the question, "Where are you from?"

Immigrants, allophones, and pretty much any others who are members of visible or religious minorities are routinely subjected to this question. It can be a well-meaning and sincere attempt to connect, to inquire about one's family history or ethnic background, and invite them to tell their story.

Or it can be an inquiry about that "foreign" name, those "ethnic" eyes or that "caramel" skin. It can feel like *othering*, categorizing someone, determining their value based on ethnicity, religion, or place of origin.

"Where are you from?" can imply that some names, skin tones, religions, and languages, do not reflect what it means to be a Canadian or a Quebecer. When respondents answer that they're from Canada or Montreal, there lurks a second question: But where are you *originally* from?

Because of that implication, asking where someone is from is a touchy question. I have heard complaints from friends who are Black, Muslims who wear the hijab, or Sikhs who wear the turban. Even if they were born and raised here, even if their families have been here for generations, they are viewed as perpetual foreigners. That stings.

In his 2021 book *Disorientation: Being Black in the World*, Canadian poet and author Ian Williams discusses how Black Canadians are often assumed to be immigrants, even though their Canadian ancestry often goes back centuries.[57] *Deeply Rooted*, a CBC documentary that traces the story of the Downey-Collins family in Nova Scotia, addresses this frustration. Even though filmmaker Cazhhmere is a seventh-generation Black Canadian with relatives who are politicians, military veterans, and boxing legends, she is constantly asked where she is from.

"On paper, my family is the most Canadian family you've ever seen," Cazhhmere says. "People have a hard time grasping the concept of someone who is not white being from Canada."[58]

She's not exaggerating. Considering how long immigrants have been part of the Canadian fabric and how quickly the demographics have been changing in larger urban cities, it seems silly to continue to make these loose assumptions.[59]

Celebrated Haitian-born writer Dany Laferrière summed it up when he observed that majority groups will claim folks as their own when it suits them, but will also be quick to denounce or dissociate from the very same group when it doesn't.

57 Ian Williams, *Disorientation: Being Black in the World*, Toronto: Penguin Random House Canada, 2021.

58 *Deeply Rooted*, directed by Cazhhmere (CBC Short Docs, 2017), https://www.cbc.ca/shortdocs/shorts/deeply-rooted.

59 Toronto is projected to be roughly 71 percent non-white by 2036; 59 percent of Montrealers were born abroad or have at least one parent who was. "Almost 7 in 10 Metro residents will be non-white in two decades," Douglas Todd, Toronto Star, May 30, 2017. Statistics Canada, Montreal Census Profile, 2016 Census.

Lorsqu'on parle des voyous de Montréal-Nord, on dit qu'ils sont Haïtiens, lorsqu'on parle de moi, on dit que je suis un grand Québécois ! Or je ne serai Québécois que lorsque tous ces voyous le seront tout autant que moi.[60]

When they talk about thugs in Montreal North, they say they're Haitian. When they talk about me, they say I'm a great Quebecer. I won't be a Quebecer until all those thugs are Quebecers too.

Even for those who otherwise fit in seamlessly, their names can betray them. As Akos Verboczy writes in *Rhapsody in Quebec*:

> "I'm Hungarian, I'm Hungarian, stop harassing me," was the cry from my everyday heart. My foreignness began to weigh on me. In the years following secondary school, I met plenty of Quebecers for whom the immigrant was still a curious beast. Being asked the same questions about my background over and over again was starting to annoy me.
>
> I would have liked to go by the name "Martin," unnoticed, to avoid provoking a barrage of questions at the beginning of any social interaction. This was rarely done out of morbid curiosity, but neither was there much genuine interest either.[61]

I often find myself stuck in the middle. I can relate to the benign curiosity and desire to connect that sometimes

---

60 Rosa Pires, "Décoloniser le « nous » de la gauche souverainiste," *Nouveaux Cahiers du socialisme* 15 (May 2016): 226.

61 Akos Verboczy, *Rhapsody in Quebec: On the Path of an Immigrant Child*, trans. Casey Roberts (Montreal: Baraka Books, 2017), 147.

inspires the question, as well as to the exasperation felt by those constantly being asked. It's the perfect example of why intention can matter more than content. *Why* the question is asked is much more important than the question itself. I've become extremely good over the years at deciphering who is engaging in what.

In a multicultural world where people navigate misconceptions, prejudices, and internalized trauma, it's important to extend some kindness and make room for the benefit of the doubt. People are still learning, still trying to become better allies, still doing the work to unlearn the assumptions of their forebears and navigate new discourses of inclusion. Patience is needed.

But not too much! Don't be too willing to brush aside obvious racism and ignorance without calling it out. There is a distinct and undeniable difference between a sincere inquiry about your cultural markers and how they may have shaped you, and the insinuation that those things make you less of a citizen.

6. An Attitude of Gratitude

You people… you come here, you love our way of
life, you love our milk and honey, at least you can
pay a couple of bucks for a poppy.

—Don Cherry

The concept of gratitude always makes an appearance in discussions of immigration, often as a weapon lobbed at those who dare criticize the society in which they live. In every debate on the subject, there is someone who pops up to let us know that they are the child of immigrants and that their parents never demanded anything when they came here.

"They came, they were grateful, they worked hard, they didn't ask for any concessions, and they taught us to work for everything we had." This is followed by a judgmental, "Not like immigrants today…"

Nothing irks me more than to see someone with a last name that clearly connotes an immigrant family making intolerant comments and engaging in selective amnesia. You, my friend, are an affront to your immigrant relatives who trudged over here and were almost certainly treated with suspicion and disdain, only to have their direct descendant treat the next wave of immigrants in the exact same way.

No, new immigrants are not *different* from the immigrants who arrived before. They are *exactly* like all other immigrants: different from the majority at the time. They don't need to "show gratitude" or "take up less space."

The requirement of gratitude hangs over the heads of immigrants and refugees like a polite request, a friendly warning, an unspoken condition, an order. Gratitude to reassure the majority that immigrants know their place. They are not to be too cocky, too arrogant, or too comfortable.

In November of 2019, right before Remembrance Day, *Hockey Night in Canada* commentator and *Coach's Corner* co-host Don Cherry went on a bizarre rant about how immigrants refuse to wear Remembrance Day poppies and honour the military.[62]

"You people…you come here, you love our way of life, you love our milk and honey, at least you can pay a couple of bucks for a poppy," he said on air, while co-host Ron MacLean silently nodded and gave the thumbs up in agreement.

You people…

The notion that immigrants snub the poppy is a powerful one. With no proof whatsoever, a well-known TV personality and someone that generations of hockey-loving Canadians grew up watching had succeeded in weaponizing Remembrance Day symbolism, draping himself in the memory of Canadian veterans in the service of xenophobia and fake patriotism.

---

62   "Don Cherry Sparks Online Backlash for Comments on Immigrants, Remembrance Day," *CBC*, November 10, 2019, https://www.cbc.ca/sports/hockey/nhl/don-cherry-sparks-online-backlash-1.5354835.

Many Canadians fell for it. What was even more painful was how many immigrants or children of immigrants felt compelled to prove Cherry wrong, flooding social media with stories of military involvement, pictures of parents or grandparents who had contributed to war efforts, or just simply offering up selfies of themselves wearing poppies. All to prove that they were Good Canadians.

The *Coach's Corner* co-host didn't deserve an answer and immigrants don't have to show proof of their love for this country, no more so than any white person with the last name Smith. Don Cherry was eventually fired because of public outrage—but a large and loyal fan base demanded his reinstatement.[63]

On June 6, 2020, Greek-Nigerian basketball player Giannis Antetokounmpo joined some of his Milwaukee Bucks teammates to march in a Black Lives Matter protest. During an interview for a documentary on *Bleacher Report*, Antetokounmpo said: "Greece is a country of whites, where the life of a man of my skin colour can be difficult. You can find yourself in different neighbourhoods and face a lot of racism."

Giannis speaks of Greece with pride and love. But it would have been a disservice to both the truth and the thousands of stateless kids who don't have the skills to

---

63 Francophones reading this will point out that Don Cherry had been spewing anti-French hate for decades and yet had been allowed to keep his job until that moment. They would be right. Cherry spent thirty years insulting francophones and francophone culture, but was never reprimanded by his bosses at CBC Television. When he was fired, few francophones in Quebec or across the country were saddened by the news. If anything, they felt his dismissal was a long time coming, and only expressed bitterness at the double standards that had allowed Cherry's anti-French bias to be amplified and normalized for so long.

become NBA superstars to refuse to discuss how racism affected his life growing up. In response to his comments, a famous mural honouring Giannis in Greece was vandalized by neo-Nazis, who painted over his face with swastikas. Konstantinos Kalemis, the coordinator for refugee education in the Malakasa camp north of Athens, tweeted that Antetokounmpo was a "monkey" and "ungrateful." The irony is palpable. He quickly deleted the "monkey" tweet when reactions got heated, but it was too late. Screenshots live on forever and outraged Greeks demanded his resignation. The Greek government promptly fired him.

While most Greeks were horrified, I also saw far too many online comments referring to "gratitude" as the reason why Giannis should have kept his mouth shut about the difficulties he experienced growing up.

Novelist Dina Nayeri, who migrated to the US as an Iranian child refugee, wrote that while it's healthy for refugees to have personal gratitude for the country that takes them in, "the expectation of gratitude is toxic."[64]

About her mother, a physician working in an American pharmaceutical factory where her far-less-educated bosses and coworkers treated her as inferior because of her accent, she writes: "From then on, we sensed the ongoing expectation that we would shed our old skin, give up our former identities—every quirk and desire that made us us—and that we would imply at

---

64   Dina Nayeri, "Expecting Gratitude from Refugees can be Toxic, Says Author," *The Current*, CBC, May 3, 2017.

every opportunity that America was better, that we were so lucky, so humbled to be here."[65]

In 2020, *Journal de Montréal* columnist Mathieu Bock-Côté provided the perfect example of this marginalizing, gratitude-demanding expectation in a column written about mayoral candidate Balarama Holness. Among Holness's electoral promises were two that rubbed the columnist the wrong way: make the city of Montreal officially bilingual, and seek city-state status for it. One has the right to disagree with a candidate's platform, but Bock-Côté spent most of his column *othering* Holness and allophones as people intent on destroying the French language and culture, and rejecting Quebec. "Some people are legitimately revolted to see that the people we welcomed here are rejecting us without shame, with uninhibited contempt," he wrote.[66]

Who is the "we" in this equation? Why is Holness, a born-and-raised Quebecer with a French Québécoise mother and a Jamaican father, not considered part of the "we"? Why did the small percentage of allophone Quebecers who supported Holness, and who may simply have different political allegiances, cease to be part of the "we"? Why were they now branded as ungrateful and perceived as the enemy, supposedly rejecting "without shame" and with "utter contempt" the place they call home? That's a lot of bad will to ascribe to a linguistic group, of which only 20 percent supported Holness at the time, and who, in a democratic society, have every right to vote for whomever they choose.

---

65   Dina Nayeri, "The Ungrateful Refugee: We Have No Debt to Repay," *The Guardian*, April 4, 2017.

66   Mathieu Bock-Côté, "Holness ne gagnera pas, mais ses idées progressent," *Journal de Montréal*, October 30, 2020.

The idea that immigrants or their children have a right to criticize social policies or government decisions, which directly affect them, their families, and their communities, seems practically anathema to some. Instead, we are seen as eternal guests, with social acceptance conditional upon our very best behaviour. Even worse, the idea that a sense of gratitude could flow in the opposite direction, *towards* newcomers, is enough to infuriate.

In early 2020, at the beginning of the COVID-19 global pandemic, Montreal was dealing with a particularly bad outbreak. The city had become the country's infection epicentre, and confirmed cases and deaths were piling up. Many of Quebec's essential workers were either testing positive for COVID-19 or were afraid to go to work because they or someone in their families were high-risk. This led to a shortage of over 11,000 workers. The situation got so dire that Premier Legault called in the Canadian Armed Forces for help in the CHSLDs, the province's public long-term care facilities.

In the midst of all this confusion was a startling fact: a disproportionate number of Quebec frontline workers who were becoming ill or dying were immigrants, a significant number of them asylum seekers who had crossed the border on foot only a few years earlier.

Many of these asylum seekers, now referred to by the premier as Quebec's "guardian angels," were desperately waiting for permanent status that would enable them to take advantage of provincial programs and services, such as free daycare for their children.

During all this, Ismaël Seck, a Quebec high-school teacher of Senegalese-Québécois origin, tweeted that he hoped Quebecers would remember the many refugees putting their lives in danger to save the province's seniors. A non-controversial sentiment, in my humble opinion. Not so for others.

Quebec French-language pundit and radio host Benoît Dutrizac immediately attacked him, calling the comment despicable and insulting towards the people who welcomed Ismaël to this province. He finished off his tweet with "Va donc chier!" in good Québécois French, telling him to basically get lost.

Two familiar things had occurred here: i) Dutrizac *othered* Seck by assuming, based on the colour of his skin and his name, that he wasn't a "real" Quebecer, and ii) as a supposed immigrant, Dutrizac believed that Seck needed to show gratitude and stay in his lane.

Used to dealing with high-school students, Seck calmly explained that he was in fact born in Quebec, and that he was simply hoping that all Quebecers would recognize the work that these refugees, so often forgotten by society, were accomplishing.

After Seck filed a complaint against Dutrizac, the radio host apologized, deleted his Twitter account, and issued a statement, saying he has "always denounced racism of all types."[67] Dutrizac later went on the radio show of Richard Martineau, a pundit equally notorious for his xenophobic and Islam-obsessed invective. Dutrizac explained that he's hot-tempered and gets riled up quickly, and it was perhaps time to take a Twitter break. He took no accountability for his actions and the so-called *mea culpa* was nothing more than a PR move, most likely demanded by his boss.

---

67   Rima Elkouri, "S'en souviendra-t-on?" *La Presse*, May 3, 2020.

Seck wasn't wrong to ask that we not lose sight of the asylum seekers working as frontline workers and their contributions to saving Quebec lives. Declarations of gratitude aside, Premier Legault wasn't willing to stick his neck out for them. When independent MNA Catherine Fournier presented a motion to grant them permanent residence, the premier would not commit to fast-tracking their applications. While Quebec's three opposition parties all voted in favour of the motion, the CAQ voted it down.

Finally, in December, 2020, when the federal government launched two special programs allowing asylum seekers who worked in the healthcare sector during the first wave of the pandemic to apply for permanent residency and gain access to the benefits that come with it, and under intense public pressure, Legault conceded— but only barely. When the Trudeau government tried to expand the program to include all asylum seekers working on the frontline during the pandemic, Quebec applied political pressure to ensure only those working in healthcare would qualify, limiting the number of refugees who would obtain permanent status.[68]

By the time the program ended on August 31, 2021, Quebec had finalized fewer than 1,500 files, far below initial projections. Immigration lawyer Stéphane Handfield called the program "disappointing," criticizing the government's bureaucracy for making applications in Quebec much more complex than in the rest of Canada.[69] Advocates for Quebec's asylum seekers

---

68   Romain Schué, "Québec finalement peu ouvert à régulariser davantage de demandeurs d'asile," *Radio-Canada*, November 20, 2020.

69   Romain Schué, "Une «ange gardien» bientôt expulsé du Canada." *Radio-Canada*, March 22, 2022.

claimed there was "no political will" or "political commitment" from the Legault government.[70] "When we die at the front lines, we're called guardian angels," Ze Benedicte Carole, an asylum seeker from Cameroon who contracted Covid-19, was reported as saying. "But when we need to be treated on an equal footing, we're not guardian angels. We're nobody, we're invisible."[71]

On the flip side of this phenomenon, immigrants who *do* display an "appropriate" amount of gratitude are described as model citizens. Pay attention the next time particular immigrants or people of colour are presented as "good immigrants." Take a closer look the next time an immigrant is given a mainstream platform to publicly praise society or the country. Yes, sometimes they are simply expressing sincere gratitude. But sometimes they are then used as a way of shutting down legitimate criticism. "Look how happy *they* are," the majority will say. "What are *you* complaining about?"

In her book, *Ne sommes-nous pas Québécoises?* Rosa Pires quotes political science professor Dimitrios Karmis, who defines colonial hospitality as "the host being generous and the immigrant as a perpetual guest, with the latter having to make all the efforts to adapt to a space that has been defined by the majority."[72]

---

70 Jacob Serebrin, "Few Quebec 'Guardian Angels' Who Worked in Health Care During Pandemic Granted Residency," *The Canadian Press*, March 24, 2021.

71 Morgan Lowrie, "Asylum Seekers Find Work in Quebec's Hard-Hit Care Homes," *The National Observer*, May 19, 2020.

72 Dimitrios Karmis, "Un couteau reste un couteau? Réflexions sur les limites de l'hospitalité québécoise," in *Du tricoté serré au métissé serré? La culture publique commune au Québec en débats*, edited by Lamoureux et. al. (Sainte-Foy : Les Presses de l'Université Laval, 2008), 255.

When people like Konstantinos Kalemis or Don Cherry or Mathieu Bock-Côté lash out at immigrants who don't display "adequate" gratitude or appear not to make sufficient effort to assimilate, what they're *really* saying is that they aren't "one of us." They are "others" who were graciously allowed into the fold and must always know their place, forever in debt to the majority, forever begging for mercy and tolerance.

Forgive me for ungraciously refusing that request.

PART TWO

7. Ode to the Second-Generation Kids

A Greek dad lying on his deathbed starts to whisper.

"Maria, my wife, are you here?"

Maria, tears streaming down her face, answers, "Yes, I'm here next to you, my love."

"My son, Giorgos, are you here?"

Giorgos answers somberly, "Yes father, I'm here."

"My daughter, Nikoleta, are you here?"

Sobbing, Nikoleta answers, "Yes, Baba, I'm here."

"My young son, Kostas, are you here?"

Kostas answers his father, "Yes, Paterouli mou (my dear dad), I'm here."

The father then sits up in his bed and says: "Then who the hell is watching the magazi (store)?"

There isn't a Greek immigrant who doesn't understand this joke.

I am a second-generation kid, a latchkey kid before there was a term for it. My parents worked such long hours that for the first decade of my life I have no memories of them relaxing at home. Opportunities to spend time together as a family were few and precious. When my father came home from work, he was so exhausted from physical labour that all I remember are frayed nerves, splayed limbs, the faintly clinging odour of fryer grease in his clothes, pizza-dough flour that floated in the air every time he attempted to brush his pant legs clean. Fatigue was palpable in the house.

My mom's trajectory in this country could be mapped out in varicose veins. Her legs are a jumble of swollen purplish-blue lines. Not the delicate branching of an errant spider vein, but the bulgy, angry kind; the kind that when I was younger I worried might burst one day and kill her. She has spent most of her working life on her feet, in Quebec *casse-croûtes* (snack bars) and diners where steamed hot dogs, French fries, and lunch specials were served all day long. She spent so much time in restaurants I sometimes think it's where she's still most comfortable. To this day, she doesn't know what to do with herself when she's not working. The kitchen, both utilitarian and comforting, is her home base. It gives her purpose and meaning.

Because my parents worked so much, I spent a lot of time on my own, playing by myself and reading book after book. My mom told me that I was a quiet kid, self-sufficient and easily left to my own devices, which was a happy coincidence because I was left to them often. I remember being far too young to be crossing streets on my own, and crossing them anyway. This streak of independence was nurtured by the absence of my parents, whether they liked it or not.

One day when I was four, I decided to go find my parents at their restaurant, about eight blocks away. I simply walked away from my babysitter, an elderly neighbour also from the south of Greece. When she couldn't locate me, the frantic lady called my mother and then the police. They soon found me, dutifully waiting for the light to turn green a few blocks away from the restaurant. I was a free bird, but I still followed traffic signals.

A few years later, when we lived in Montreal's east end, my parents co-owned a huge restaurant on Sherbrooke Street. At the front was a high-end dining room, at the back a casual diner. I went there most days after school, passing through the fancy section, coming across my dad in the kitchen who would urge me to sample frogs' legs and escargot or whatever dish a seven-year-old has no use for, and make my way to the back. School books tucked under my arm, I would settle into an impossibly cozy diner booth and do my homework. My mom would come by, ask me what I wanted to eat and leave a bunch of shiny quarters on the table for the jukebox. I would listen to whichever pop song had caught my attention— often in repetition, to everyone's dismay. Dinner consisted of hot dogs smothered in mustard, or a grilled cheese sandwich, or whatever was the *spécial du jour*. I ate all-dressed pizza and shepherd's pie and smoked meat sandwiches, all staples of Montreal Greek diners. For dessert, the waitresses knew to bring me a slice of lemon meringue pie or creamy rice pudding with extra cinnamon. It was a routine that repeated itself almost daily for years.

My mother is a phenomenal cook. She makes traditional Greek food the way it's supposed to be made— generously greasy and heavy on the oil—and her *avgolemono* (egg-lemon chicken soup) would be my choice for last meal were I ever on death row. And yet, it wasn't until I was eleven, when my parents sold their business and we moved to Greece, that I got to enjoy my mother's home cooking. There, for the first time, I had the pleasure of a stay-at-home mom who had the time and the luxury to cook for us.

Before that, the hours they worked running and managing their restaurants required a price, and that price was exacted from their family. I loved them and was loved by them, but I learned to live largely without them growing up. When my sister came along, my mom would rely on me, barely ten years old, to babysit. While I did this for free, my eight-year-old brother was paid a dollar to behave and not cause me any grief. I came by my feminism early.

This left-to-my-own-devices life was all I and many other second-generation children knew. A good friend of mine, whose Chinese parents owned a noodle factory, used to joke that today our parents would be thrown in jail for neglect. Having shouldered responsibilities at such a young age themselves, our parents didn't think twice about our ability to do the same. And yet, we never doubted that we were ferociously loved.

Second-generation kids whose working-class parents had a limited education and didn't easily acquire second-language skills are different from other kids. Particularly the eldest ones. We're bill readers, doctor's-appointment-makers, bank-statement decryptors, de facto translators for all things major and minor, and we had no one to help with our homework because our parents didn't have enough schooling or enough knowledge of English or French to be of any assistance.

Second-generation kids are old beyond our years, responsible for things we shouldn't be responsible for, made aware of things we sometimes shouldn't have had to be. We're cultural ambassadors, conscripted to bridge the familiar and the foreign.

Second-generation kids are also often the first ones to go to college. We enter educational institutions our parents will never set foot in. We experience the isolation of not being able to share our academic successes and career achievements with our parents. My parents have always known I wrote, yet they have never read a single one of my columns. My mother will never read this book.

They've seen my byline and the picture that accompanies it. They understand the concept of my vocation, but their rudimentary English language skills and inability to fully understand what I do keeps me forever apart from them. I have come to terms with this but it's a lonely feeling, alleviated only by the fact that I know I'm not the only one who's experienced it.

Out of everything I've ever accomplished in my career, the one milestone they were most able to identify with and be proud of was my two-year stint co-hosting *Hellas Spectrum*, a Montreal-based, nationally broadcast Greek television program. It was a fun experience and I enjoyed working with and interviewing members of Montreal's Greek community, but I'd hardly consider it the highlight of my career. And, yet…Greek folks in the community still stop me and ask me why I haven't been "on TV lately" even though, by my calculations, my last appearance co-hosting that show was roughly eight or nine years ago.

That was the only accomplishment my parents could understand—literally, because it was in Greek. Their friends in the community could comment on it. It felt like success. It was something they could appreciate, gloat about, share with others, and be proud of. The other stuff, well, it had no real meaning or importance in their own lives.

Award-winning writer Junot Díaz, talking at a Blue Metropolis Literary Festival event in 2015, told the audience that his mother "doesn't give a fuck about a Pulitzer." The crowd roared with laughter, but he was being deadly serious. As an immigrant kid, I knew exactly what he meant. A Pulitzer is not something an uneducated immigrant woman from the Dominican Republic would covet or understand. Her aspirations for her son boiled down to how much money his writing had made him.

Along similar lines, Tina Vasquez, a US-based assistant research director and journalist who writes about migration and immigration policies at a social-justice think tank (try explaining that to first-generation parents!), tweeted out this little gem in 2019: "My grandpa recently told me I should move back to Los Angeles because the *L.A. Times* is looking for people to deliver the paper. 1. I don't drive. 2. Has my grandpa spent the last 10+ years thinking I "deliver" the news, like literally?"

I laughed out loud because I know that if my parents or grandparents had been forced to explain exactly what I do for a living, they would have also given some rudimentary description that barely approximated how I pay my bills. Their reference points simply don't include bylines or pull quotes.

My father was consumed with work. It's all he'd ever known. You don't come to the new country and not take advantage of the opportunities given to you. Also, when you had little at the start of your life, you never stop looking for financial security, enough to take care of yourself and your family. My parents didn't squander money on luxuries or frills.

Most of that generation did little else but work. First-generation immigrants *still* do nothing but work, usually at jobs no one else wants. A few years ago, I was a freelance news producer for a morning television show. The alarm would go off at 2:30 a.m. and I would soon be in the back of a cab, rolling along Montreal's eerily quiet streets in the darkness of early morning towards our downtown studios. There's something very intimate about two strangers alone in a car while the rest of the city sleeps. Secrets and jokes are shared, a trust develops. I never felt scared or vulnerable during those late-night rides while I coaxed my body to wake up. On the contrary, I often thought of how vulnerable a taxi driver is, back to a stranger, exposed to their whims, their possible prejudice, even their physical violence. More recently, exposed to a deadly virus.[73]

Two things were constants: the driver would immediately assume I was on my way home after a late night (which was entertaining, considering my club-hopping years were long behind me), and the driver would be a recent immigrant.

No one does the graveyard shift unless they have to.

---

73 Jessica Patton, "10 Airport Taxi, Limo Drivers Have Died Since Beginning of Coronavirus Pandemic, Union Says," *Global News*, May 6, 2020.

I've spoken to taxi drivers who work through the night only to go home, take a quick shower, and then head out to university where they pursue their studies and a new future. Accounting, public policy, architecture, business—they rattle off the degrees they're working on. Nothing is too far out of reach; nothing is too difficult to try. I'm in awe of their work ethic, their determination, and their unyielding optimism. A jovial taxi driver of Pakistani origin once switched to impeccable Greek (not an easy language to learn) upon hearing where I was from. Having worked for years alongside Greeks in the restaurant industry, he had picked up the language. We continued the rest of the ride in Greek and I left the cab marvelling at people's ability to soak up everything around them. Here was a man who had not only learned French upon arriving in Quebec, but had managed to pick up a completely useless (in terms of financial value) language simply because he was interested. This was not exactly the stereotype of immigrants being resistant towards or unable to acquire a new culture.

While in Greece in the summer of 2018, I found myself talking to taxi drivers there too, many of them also immigrants. In a cab to the airport for my return flight to Montreal, my Albanian driver appeared to be in his late sixties. He told me how he had crossed the Greek border fourteen times and was deported fourteen times.

"Each time I would return," he said with a playful wink.

He finally managed to get through. He's been in Greece for twenty-nine years, consistently working and raising a family. He took out his wallet at a red light and, beaming with pride, showed me a picture of his youngest daughter who had just been accepted to medical school. I smiled back. I was his daughter too. I'm that second generation who benefited from the first generation's sacrifices and risk-taking. I'm the second generation that had it a little easier, slept a little sounder, dreamed a little bigger.

Gracia Kasoki Katahwa made Montreal municipal history by being elected mayor of Montreal's largest borough, Côte-des-Neiges—Notre-Dame-de-Grâce, becoming the first Black female borough mayor. She spoke of her father during her acceptance speech. I teared up while watching. Katahwa, who grew up in the Democratic Republic of Congo in a family of modest means, described the moment she told him she would be entering politics to run for borough mayor. There was a long pause from her father on the other end of the line, she said.

"A silence that expressed the long obstacle course that is immigration—the wins, the losses, the resilience and the overwhelming emotion that comes from seeing that your efforts bear fruit."[74]

Kasoki Katahwa wasn't an outlier. In 2021, a record number of new Montreal borough councillors were second-generation immigrants, representing diverse communities which, in the past, didn't have a seat at the table. Now, feet firmly planted in this place, they were giving back. That included their children, who now had deep roots in this place, running for political office. Among them, Stéphanie Valenzuela, the very first Filipina Canadian to ever be elected to Montreal City

---

74   Verity Stevenson, "Gracia Kasoki Katahwa Wins Nail-Biter in Côte-des-Neiges—Notre-Dame-de-Grâce," *CBC News*, November 8, 2021.

Council, who stated that her win "was a privilege and a reminder every day of the sacrifices my parents made to give my sister and myself a better life."[75]

Across the river from Montreal, on the South Shore, the new political party Coalition Longueuil, led by former PQ MNA Catherine Fournier, also elected a number of diverse candidates—Rolande Balma, Alvaro Cueto, Affine Lwalalika, Lysa Bélaïcha—all children of immigrants.

"We represent the Quebec in which we live," says Lysa Bélaïcha, born in Algeria twenty-two years ago, arriving in Quebec at the age of three. "Yes, I'm black, but I'm from Quebec," adds Rolande Balma, twenty-one years old, who arrived from Burkina Faso in 2014.

"They have one thing in common with their colleagues Affine Lwalalika, originally from the Democratic Republic of Congo, and Alvaro Cueto, born here to Chilean parents: the four are in love with Quebec. Their neighbourhood. Their city. The French language. They feel at home and want to 'give back' to their neighbours."[76]

I'm not objective, I admit it. As a second-generation immigrant, I will be forever in awe of the resilience and drive possessed by first generation individuals who often face tremendous adversity. It doesn't matter how ardently some try to prevent them from starting a new life, they start it anyway.

---

75 "Montreal's First Filipina City Councillor," *CityNews Montreal*, November 12, 2021, https://montreal.citynews.ca/video/2021/11/12/montreals-first-filipina-city-councillor/.

76 Lise-Marie Gervais and Marco Fortier, "Les élections de la diversité," *Le Devoir*, November 9, 2021.

When my dad retired, he didn't know what to do with himself. Having never cultivated a hobby or outside interests, I worried that he was lost without a purpose. Nothing had equipped my parents to seek out entertainment, travel, or education to fill the gap after retirement. Only manual labour seemed to give my dad a purpose. It's why he enjoyed puttering around for hours in his orange grove in Greece, and why old Italian men in the suburb of Rivière des Prairies produce enough Roma tomatoes to supply the entire neighbourhood. It gives them a sense of accomplishment and mastery. More importantly, they can't sit still.

The only time they do is when they gather for coffee and have something to talk about. Pay attention the next time you're in a suburban shopping mall food court, a McDonald's, or an Italian, Middle Eastern or Greek café. You'll see immigrant senior men gather every day at the same spot, nursing a cup of coffee, arguing loudly about politics back home, reminiscing about the old days, or informing each other about the latest member of the community to pass away.

"May his memory be eternal."

"Life is so short."

"We blinked and it's over."

"What did we accomplish?"

"Who will even remember us?"

"Make sure Maria knows I want to be buried in Greece..."

All parents and children are already worlds apart. But immigrant parents and second-generation kids can be universes apart. The kids are often caught between old-school immigrant parents ordering, guilting, or shaming them into following cultural traditions and religion, and their own desire to shed what they see as restrictive cultural baggage. Allophones navigate and negotiate multiple identities, languages, and traditions, some days without even leaving the house.

I wouldn't change anything about being a second-generation immigrant. It has unequivocally made me who I am today: someone with extra layers of understanding and empathy for the different, the new, and the marginalized, and an ability to see things from multiple points of view. My identity as the child of immigrants has shaped me as a writer, a journalist and, most importantly, as a human being. Being raised by people who had to journey through a world and a culture that made little room for them has given me a perspective that enables me to easily put myself in others' shoes. That is a priceless gift, one for which I will be forever grateful.

8. Surviving, Not Writing

Ever since I can remember, there has been a book in my hand. I'm a voracious reader and books have kept me company, been a source of constant wonderment, and guarded my sanity. I can't imagine life without them. Even now, as an adult with conflicting deadlines and goals, I often read two or three books at a time. One of my biggest regrets is that I will not have the time to discover even more literary worlds.

No one in my immediate family reads for pleasure, and I don't recall any books in our home. I didn't come to books because someone told me I should read or even because I saw other people reading. Quite the opposite.

Once, when I was in my room as a young teen, completely immersed in a novel, my dad passed by and asked if I was reading for school. Barely looking up from the book, I told him no. He replied, "So, why are you reading it?" It was a sincere question from a simple man who saw books only as a means to good grades and an education. He couldn't fathom why his teenage daughter was reading in a dark room while it was gorgeously sunny outside. If you weren't reading to advance your studies to ensure a good life, then what was the point?

I never forgot that encounter. It was one of many little hints that revealed I was different from my parents and probably always would be. That there were some things we would never see eye to eye on. We would have a parallel existence where blood and love would keep us tied together, but we would never quite meet.

And yet, this man would fork over his hard-earned money to get me the entire Encyclopedia Britannica set when a travelling salesman (remember them?) showed up at our door. To my dad, who only had a fifth-grade education, those heavy, leather-bound volumes signified some level of financial and social success. Because he could see the hunger in my eyes, and because he wanted me to have a leg up in this world, my father bought them all. I spent hours sitting on the floor reading and marvelling at a world I would one day get to see and experience. That gift meant everything to me. It still does.

Books saved me. Reading allowed me to make sense of the world and I took to it like a fish to water. My teachers had to tell me to slow down when I read out loud. Reading, particularly for a quiet kid who spent many hours alone, was solace and companionship. I went through every single Nancy Drew mystery, and then, when those adventures ran out, I turned to the Hardy Boys for more sleuthing. The world needed to be solved and I was on the case! Reading was also knowledge. At age eight my library card was my most prized possession. Even though I continue to spend a small fortune on books, my library card is my saving grace as I try to minimize damage to my crowded bookshelves and my credit card. I consider libraries one of the most vital democratic institutions of our time. They provide a door that would never otherwise be open to worlds beyond experience, and my gratitude for them knows no bounds.

Even when we moved to Greece when I was eleven—
or maybe *because* we moved to Greece—I found myself
relying on books once again to show me the way, into a
new community, a new language, and a new collection
of reference points. I devoured our town's small library.
I was that teenager who could be found on the beach
reading Simone de Beauvoir's *The Second Sex* or modern Greek authors like Nikos Kazantzakis and Menelaos
Lountemis; a book about the Nazi occupation one day
and some cheesy Harlequin romance the next. Nothing
would be left unread.

Despite my love for words and writing (the first thing
a former grade four classmate said when she was asked
what she remembered about me was that I was always
scribbling stories in my notebooks) I never contem-
plated being a writer.

Second-generation kids must contend with the
expectations of their immigrant parents. In many cases,
not only are we the first generation to attain a higher
education, we are also steered away from fields such as
the arts, which are not considered respectable. If I was
good with words, it stood to reason that I was destined
to become a lawyer. Since I excelled in school, it went
without saying that I would become a doctor— at the
very least, a pharmacist or a dentist. For the love of
God...perhaps a notary?

During an interview, comedian Hannah Gadsby
asked writer Roxane Gay if she always knew that she
wanted to be a writer. "Always," Gay replied. "From four
years old, I knew. Which is good, but also bad, especially
with immigrant parents, who are just like, what? No.
You're going to be a lawyer, doctor, or engineer, which

is the Haitian trifecta of careers. It was hard. They supported my writing, always, but they didn't understand that it's what I wanted to do full-time. They were being realistic, and I was being a dreamer, and so I understand where they were coming from. But I always just believed that I could make a go of it."[77]

Immigrant parents often don't have the luxury of dreams. Theirs is an optimistic pragmatism. Impractical professions like art and literature are frowned upon and offspring are encouraged to study medicine, law, engineering, or accounting—professions that are always in demand and come with solid earning potential and elevated social status. Immigrant parents encourage their kids to avoid the trades or following in the family business, which for my parents' generation was often the restaurant industry. They don't want their kids to go through what they went through.

My parents, and many other first-generation parents, who came here from poverty-stricken, war-torn countries, with limited educations and laser-focused aspirations, were products of their time and of their circumstances. If they veered towards the practical career paths, it's because the world taught them to do so. It's hard to muse philosophically or ponder the universe when you're starving or dodging bullets. It's hard to put down prose or compose music when you don't know where your next meal is coming from or you've been doing manual labour since 5:00 a.m. Being an artist often means your basic needs have been met and your problems are first-world problems. It's the second- and

77 Rebecca Nicholson, "Hannah Gadsby Meets Roxane Gay," *The Guardian*, December 8, 2018.

third-generation kids that get to dream. Who you are is a product of not only your interests and intellect, but also your circumstances.

In the summer of 2021, on my first trip after eighteen months of pandemic-limited contact with the world, I found myself on the Greek island of Hydra, where Montreal-born Leonard Cohen had spent almost seven years of his life living and writing in the 60s. As an avid Cohen fan, I rejoiced at my time there, visiting his home and all his famous haunts on the island. It felt like a pilgrimage of sorts and it gave me immense joy to walk the cobbled streets and alleyways he had walked, stroll the beaches where he had swum, sit at Douskos Taverna where LIFE photographer James Burke snapped those now-iconic images of him and his bohemian crew.

While reading many articles about his time there, I came across one where the author stated that Leonard and his fellow creatives had been "brave" to come to Hydra in the 60s. I shared the quote with my travelling companion, also the daughter of immigrants, and we both chuckled. What, pray tell, was brave about lounging around on a gorgeous Greek island, spending summer days and nights in a paradise with an expat community of like-minded artists? What's so brave about choosing austerity when you know you can leave it all behind at the drop of a hat? I'm not minimizing Cohen's decision to live without the comforts of home, sweltering in the summer months and freezing in the damp winters. Their lifestyle was indeed simple and they probably made do with little. But it was still a safe *choice*. As they were basking in their creative utopia on Hydra, my parents were fighting to build a new life and working fourteen-hour shifts in a city where they didn't speak the language and barely knew a soul.

Brave is taking the leap when you have no safety net. No inheritance from your grandmother to buy an island home for yourself, no Canada Council writing grants, no rich family in Westmount to bail you out. While privileged young bohemians were congregating on Hydra in the 60s, thousands of Greeks were boarding ships headed in the other direction. Unfortunately, they didn't have a minute to spare to contemplate life's beauty and complexity, let alone pen a song or poem about it.

When I think back to the hours my dad worked, the varicose veins that colonized my mom's legs, the exhaustion on their faces, it's only natural that they would measure success by how much easier our lives would be. They didn't cross oceans and develop calluses the size of garbanzo beans so we could play penniless *artiste* or enter a profession that might not exist in ten years.

And yet, despite the obstacles, diasporas have produced a wealth of art and literature with its own spin on otherness and belonging. It's what writer Salman Rushdie refers to as the writing of the "plural and partial."[78] We are here to offer our own take on things and add to the ever-expanding literature of our home.

---

78 Salman Rushdie, *Imaginary Homelands* (London: London Review of Books, 1982).

9. Shifting Loyalties

My integration as an immigrant child passed
through the shame of what I was, the rejection of
who I was, and a series of small betrayals of myself
and my parents.

—Caroline Dawson, *Là où je me terre*

An immigrant exists in a state of multiple identities and
shifting loyalties. The mere act of integration requires
that a transformation take place. You're not only leading
a different life from the one you would have had back in
the "old country," you're leading a double life. You're one
person in public, another at home. At home, you speak
another language, are often called by another name, and
are seen as someone else. The term "third culture" has
sometimes been used to describe the unique perspective
that someone can have in a new country. You are not
enough *us* and too much *other*.

Greek Canadians are Greek and they are Canadian.
Even more, they are the combination of the two. How
they identify and how they end up labelling themselves
depends on the strength and influence of each of the
various parts of their personas. For some, Greek identity overrides everything. You know the type: Greek flag
in the window, a tattoo of the *300*, worry beads in the

car, doesn't marry outside of the community, teaches the kids to speak Greek. It matters immensely to them.

For others, they are Canadians (or Quebecers) first and their Greekness is just added flavouring, something to trot out during family gatherings, weddings, or national holidays. A lovely addition to their lives, memories of Greek school, that summer vacation they take every few years, but it's the sideshow, not the main act.

Every time I pass by some of the remaining few Greek associations on Park Avenue, the area simply referred to as "*ta Parkaveneika*" by my dad, I can't help but hear the voices of the elderly folks on the association boards.

"Come by one afternoon," they plead. "We need more young people on the board." To no avail. Most of the younger generation is busy. While many of us may enjoy the annual festivals, dances, and fundraisers, and get involved in local Greek community affairs, concerns about language and religion simply aren't a priority. Despite the majority's concerns about new immigrants not adapting to local norms, I'm here to tell you integration works. Some might say it works too well.

Immigrants can be accused of not assimilating quickly enough; of creating and maintaining cultural ghettos. But what outsiders see is most often just a single generation's trajectory. Newcomers congregate in their own communities because there's a comfort in being around people who understand you—not only linguistically. It can be mentally exhausting and physically gruelling to be constantly questioned, mistrusted, or even feared, all while navigating new languages, customs, and social mores in an unfamiliar landscape.

But the transition eventually happens. It's why, after living in homogenous communities, immigrants eventually spread out, and purchase homes and businesses outside of their ethnic enclaves. Their children, who now identify mostly as Canadian, go where they please. While their culture and language are still important, proximity to people of the same background is no longer a necessity. I don't know how many Greeks live in my neighbourhood of Saint-Henri and, frankly, I don't care.

Montreal's Jean-Talon West is the stretch where Greek bakeries share space with Indian and Pakistani restaurants, halal grocery stores, Black-owned hair salons, and convenience stores selling British beer and Bollywood videos. Waves of history are visible via the stores and the old men resting on the benches.

A few classic Greek establishments remain. Village Grec still serves gyro pitas; Panama and Marvin's still dole out mouth-watering grilled meat, lemony oven-roasted potatoes and side orders of garlicky tzatziki; and Afroditi Bakery still has a loyal clientele coming by for the melomakarouna (honey cookies) or the Easter tsoureki (sweet braided bread). The Koimisis Tis Theotokou Greek Orthodox Church—referred to simply and lovingly as Panagitsa (Little Mother Mary) in the neighbourhood—on St. Roch still brings in the faithful. And Jean-Talon still closes to traffic for the three-day festival on August 15th to honour the Virgin Mary. But now, when I come to Jean-Talon, I'm usually in the neighbourhood to get my eyebrows threaded or to eat at Bombay Mahal, my favourite Indian BYOB.

The Park Ex (Park Extension) neighbourhood is no longer solely Greek. These days, the Pakistani, Indian,

African, Caribbean, and Latin-American communities have moved in and that's all right with me. That's how it works with gateway neighbourhoods. They are the landing pads that welcome new immigrants with limited means, sending them off to greener pastures a generation or two later. By the time members of Montreal's Greek community had enough money to commission statues like The Greek Immigrant at the corner of Jean-Talon and Park, most of them had already moved on to suburbs in Laval or the South Shore.

The word *diaspora* is derived from the ancient Greek word that means to scatter. Immigrants scatter around the world to new homes, and then continue to scatter even within countries to new cities, different communities.

In the process, not only does culture shift, but so too do allegiances. Chilean-Québécois author Caroline Dawson describes the moment she realized she had replaced her mother tongue with French when, as a young mother, she had no Spanish lullabies to sing to her baby.[79] Rosa Pires describes how her sense of belonging to Portugal was not so different from how she felt about weekends spent at a Quebec chalet. It tinted her view of the world, but it was a sentiment she associated with the "lightness of vacations, comfortable and welcoming."[80] When Greek Canadians, who only know Greece from summer vacations, tell me that they want to move there permanently because "life is better," I'm tempted to remind them that life is better anywhere you're on

---

79 Caroline Dawson, *Là où je me terre*, (Montréal: Les Éditions du remue-ménage, 2020), 189.

80 Pires Rosa, *Ne Sommes-Nous Pas Québécoises*, (Montréal: Les Éditions du remue-ménage, 2019), 42.

vacation. They don't know Greece, they only know the highlight reel. But that too shapes who they are and how they see themselves.

Here's what happens if, like me, you're the type that floats effortlessly between two (or even more) worlds and does not privilege either: while your community's elders bemoan the slow but steady erosion of language and customs, the larger society will congratulate you for passing as one of them. In the end, you will never be enough for either. You will learn to live in this no man's land that has ever-shifting borders and you will never be sure which side will generate the attack, the guilt trip, and the reproach.

While you're being criticized from within your community for not being enough, you will also bear the burden of representing "your" people outside of the compound. This is something that most members of the majority will never have to experience.

The minute someone is arrested or convicted of murder or anything else that's illegal or morally shameful, the first thing immigrants or religious minorities do is check the person's name. If it's obviously Greek or Italian or Muslim, they think, "Great. It had to be one of us."

It would never even occur to a member of a majority to feel discomfort at the thought of one of their own misrepresenting them. White men aren't collectively blamed for the actions of individual white men, even though statistically they comprise the overwhelming majority of violent criminals. Christians aren't blamed for the actions of some Christians, even though the world's colonizing was often done in their god's name. Yet Muslims are all blamed for the actions of some Muslims, and so called Black-on-Black crime is used as an example of the "hopelessness" of that community.

Minorities self-censor and self-regulate. *"What will people say?"* is a question often asked by chastising parents, but never more so than by ethnic parents. Minorities feel the full weight of that duty of representation.

In his 2004 book *Limbo: Blue-Collar Roots, White-Collar Dreams*, award-winning journalist Alfred Lubrano talks about how hard-working first-generation university graduates find themselves straddling both blue-collar and white-collar worlds, feeling like they don't belong in either. The son of a Brooklyn bricklayer, Lubrano sat in class at Columbia University while his father was laying bricks at a nearby campus building.[81]

To straddle two or three different worlds at once—to have a "limbo identity"—is exhausting. Upward mobility of any kind creates both opportunity and ambivalence for the people living it. A sense of pride and tenacity can often be found side by side with survivor guilt, shame, profound insecurity, and a lack of confidence.

Lubrano talks of feeling like a fish-out-of-water, never completely comfortable in either world. I know that feeling well. It took me years to stop believing that I was only impersonating a writer, instead of actually being one. I continue to remind myself when doubt creeps in: I'm not the only one. There are thousands and perhaps millions of us around the world.

---

81 Alfred Lubrano, *Limbo: Blue-Collar Roots, White-Collar Dreams*, (New Jersey: Wiley, 2005), 16.

10. English, Frenglish, Greeklish

> To say what you want to say, you must create
> another language and nourish it for years with
> what you have loved, with what you have lost, with
> what you will never find again.
>
> —George Seferis

Language is more than just communication. It is how we acquire, carry, and pass down what defines us and what we value. Our mother tongue…*la langue maternelle*… *mitriki glossa*. Even the expression "mother tongue" implies its transmission since birth; some scientists claim even while we're *in* the womb.

If you're the daughter of immigrants, your parents will most likely want you to learn their language. Growing up, I was a Canadian kid, doing Canadian things, going to Canadian school. But on Saturday morning, when most of my classmates got to watch cartoons, I was trucked off to Greek school. Decades later, I still remember my annoyance and my parents' attempts to barter outings or the approval I craved as a second-generation Greek. No matter how many hours my parents worked, no matter how much they would have appreciated one less car trip, Greek school wasn't up for discussion. Every Saturday morning, they would drive me to Holy Trinity Church, at the corner of Sherbrooke and Clark, the oldest Greek Orthodox Church in Montreal.

There, I and other young Greek-Canadian kids were taught our history, culture, and religion. The lessons were rudimentary and, in retrospect, full-on indoctrination. But it was mostly about the language.

I love language, especially when it is precise and economical. I love its fluidity and beauty, its capacity to communicate emotions and desires. I love that it is constantly evolving, and forever changing.

Language can also be tricky. In Quebec, we live with cultural insecurity about the survival of French in the province. I love living in a city where French and English play together as *franglais* and form new, different words that only mean something to those who live here. Within this city, and throughout the Greek diaspora, we, too, have invented new words that mean something only to us. While the purists agonize, many of us revel in the discovery of a secret language for the here and now.

Code-switching, defined as alternating between two or more languages or varieties of language, is something most second-generation kids do without even noticing. I can start a sentence in English, switch to Greek, and finish in French. Some second-generation immigrants are even able to switch between the less complex, "broken" form of the majority language spoken (the one their parents often speak) and the intricate "proper" form they engage in for everyday use. Chinese-American author, Amy Tan, writes, "Language is the tool of my trade. And I use them all—all the Englishes I grew up with."[82]

82   Amy Tan, "Mother Tongue," *The Threepenny Review*, No. 43 (1990): 7-8.

Some people consider code-switching a substandard form of communication, and while being able to switch in and out of the dominant language is a survival mechanism (for example, Black people dropping their African-American Vernacular English, commonly known as Ebonics, or people with regional or class accents adopting more standard forms), it's mostly just the brain being comfortable with multiple forms of speech. Most multilingual people engage in this behaviour and the ability to do so becomes an integral part of their identity. People offended by code-switching aren't interested in language, they're interested in *policing* language.

Only members of the Greek diaspora speak Greeklish. The words are not in a Greek dictionary and no one who lives in Greece would have a clue what you were talking about. These hybrid words, which in some cases evolve into a patois or even a pidgin language, speaks to the presence of a geographically and socio-culturally defined mode of communication within a unique community. You often don't know where one language ends and the other begins.

There is an entire vocabulary created by Greek Canadians clumsily attaching vowels to English and French words in an effort to Hellenize them. The linguistic term for such a procedure is "lexical borrowing." This hybrid language is often considered to be normal by the younger generation—who eventually travel to Greece on summer vacation only to discover they're speaking gibberish no one outside of Canada understands.

It's said that more than 150,000 English words (mostly technical and scientific terms) are derived from Greek. (The fictional dad from my *Big Fat Greek Wedding*,

Gus Portokalos, would claim that *all* words are derived from Greek.) But Greek immigrants somehow felt compelled to invent a few more. Boy, did they come up with some doozies! In the deep of winter, I would hear my dad moan about the weather and the *bilozeria* we were subjected to. "This is a country only suited to bears!" he would say after shovelling snow off the stairs for the third time. *Bilozeria* is Greeklish for *below zero*.

Greek Canadians (particularly those of my parents' generation who had a limited education) don't say car or even *autokinito*. They say *caro*. They don't say either cheque or *trapeziki epitagi*, they say *tseki*. The shopping is done at the *marketa*. *Bosis* is a boss, *stofa* is a stove, *friza* is a fridge, *flori* is a floor, *hoteli* is a hotel. In most cases, a Greek suffix is added to simply make an English word look and sound Greek. Street names get the same treatment. *Zantalo* is Jean-Talon, *Salora* is St. Laurent, and *ta Parkaveneika* is the Park Avenue area.

The use of Greeklish in the Greek-Montreal community can lead to entertaining anecdotes. I remember my aunt sending my brother and me Christmas cards one year with some money enclosed. In them, she had written Μέρες Κρίσιμες, instead of the Greek wish for Merry Christmas, Καλά Χριστούγεννα. If you read it phonetically, *Meres krisimes* sounds very much like Merry Christmas. However, written with Greek characters it literally means Days of Crisis. My brother and I laughed for a long time over that one.

When my dad would lose patience, he would often say, "Είμαι Ζαμαφουτιστας!" (*ime zamafoutistas*). I had no idea what he was talking about. It was only years later that I came to the surprising realization that he was speaking a Greeklish version of the French phrase *Je m'en fous*, which essentially translates as, "I don't give a damn!"

Languages feed off one another. There are hundreds of Turkish words sprinkled throughout the Greek language. How could there not be? Four hundred years of Ottoman occupation will do that, even in a country that fought hard to preserve its language and religion. Many common Greek words and expressions are derived from Turkish, such as *i sihtir* (get out of here), *kafetzis* (café owner), or *karpouzi* (watermelon). Likewise, many Turkish words are Greek in origin, for example *efenti* for boss is derived from the Greek *afentis*. Going in the other geographical direction, the Greek word for couch, *kanape*, made its way to France and became canapé, something you eat…on a couch.

What's the commonly used Greek word for elevator? *Asanser,* which is nothing more than the Greek pronunciation of the French word *ascenseur*. Do you know the popular Greek word that describes the English slang that younger generations routinely inject into their speech? *Argot*. Only, it's not a Greek word, or even an English word. It's a French word. The Greeks use a French word to identify the infiltration of English words into the Greek vocabulary! Does any of this make sense? No, not really. There is no bigger thief than language.

Here in Quebec, especially in multicultural and multilingual Montreal, it's perfectly normal that Franglais—a mashup of French and English—has emerged. It doesn't mean that most people using it don't know how to properly use either French or English, it means they enjoy speaking Franglais and it feels perfectly natural to them to combine the two. Many Quebec rappers—such as the Dead Obies, Alaclair Ensemble, and Loud Lary Ajust—use Franglais in their music..It hasn't earned them any love from language purists, but their young fans enjoy it and see it as a way to bridge cultural divides.[83]

Rappelle-toi qu'on est parti de nothing

Pis que ma moms work à l'usine sur le nightshift

—"Montréal Sud," Dead Obies

I understand that lyrics like this might not be for everyone. But language goes where it wants. People are afraid that Franglais will affect the quality of spoken French or undermine the language's survival, but that theory doesn't hold up.[84] After all, isn't it perfectly normal that two linguistic communities living side by side will alter and colour each other's languages? How could they not?

Italian Quebecer Marco Micone, a playwright and essayist, often had his characters speaking a hybrid language, one that included words like *Sacraminte*, the Italian version of the popular Québécois swear word *Sacrament*.

In some instances, entirely new words are invented. My Italian brother-in-law who hails from Toronto has often used the term *"mangiacake."* It is a derogatory term used by blue-collar Italian Canadians to describe WASPs, and has evolved to include Italian Canadians

---

83 Huw Oliver, "Parlez-vous Franglais? Montreal's Bilingual Rappers Speak their Own Language," *The Guardian*, September 17, 2015.

84 "University of Ottawa Study Suggests Franglais Isn't Weakening French," *CBC News*, February 7, 2018.

who have thoroughly assimilated. They have now become full-on white-bread-eating white people.

It is most often in multicultural and multilingual cities that people borrow each other's languages as their traditions, dialects, cuisine, and other markers of identity share space and occasionally clash. Eventually, some immigrants start to resemble the majority more than the minority group from which they originated. It's a dilution of sorts, but it's also an expansion, a spreading out into something new.

11. Halifax: A Clash of Allegiance

Nothing illustrates my multiple identities like the jumble of emotions I felt visiting Nova Scotia in 2019. I had been wanting to go to the Canadian Museum of Immigration at Pier 21 in Halifax for years. The original building my parents, and most mid-century immigrants to Canada, came through was transformed by the Canadian government into a museum honouring immigrant history and its importance to this country's legacy. I wanted to see where it all began and add a visual to the stories my parents shared with me.

By Montreal standards, Halifax is a sleepy port town. With a population of 413,000, it still has a small-town vibe and the warmth that the Maritimes are known for. Facing the Halifax harbour, the museum's cavernous building by the pier looks quite ordinary. I don't know what I expected, to be honest. It's not like neon lights are usually involved in most of our milestones and it's not like a pier in eastern Canada was ever supposed to be that transformational.

The Halifax harbour is, after Sydney's in Australia, the second deepest harbour in the world. This depth is what prevents it from freezing during winter, allowing ships to dock throughout the year, making it an active trade and immigration hub. There's something magical about a port so deep that it can keep welcoming hopes and dreams, Canadian winters be damned.

The reception hall where immigrants were first received by government workers has not been renovated much. The floor is the exact same floor my parents walked on when they first landed. I was surprised to catch myself becoming emotional, literally walking in my parents' footsteps. How were they greeted? What were they thinking? What were they afraid of, hoping for, amazed by?

In room after room, moving testimonials from decades of immigration are on display, accompanied by black and white pictures of real people who built real lives. I see it all on their faces. Hesitation and fatigue, hope and possibility, joy and trepidation. This nondescript building feels like a sacred place.

Through the floor-to-ceiling windows, one sees, facing the harbour, Georges Island. Named after George II of Great Britain, this pretty little spot is where Acadians were imprisoned during the nine years of the Acadian Expulsion (1755-64). Fort Charlotte, on the island, was the site of imprisonment, military activity, and executions. My parents knew none of that.

I, however, do.

The Acadian Expulsion was the forced deportation of the French-speaking citizens of what are now Nova Scotia, New Brunswick, and Prince Edward Island by British soldiers during the Seven Years' War between England and France. Wanting no part of the war, the Acadians had signed an oath of neutrality and declared no allegiance to either side. This made them enemies of the Crown.

After the deportation, approximately ten to eleven thousand Acadians found themselves without a home.

Many of the refugees fled to Louisiana (to what is now known as Cajun country), Quebec, the colonies of what is now New England, or the Caribbean. Many others perished in squalid conditions on the ships—dying of exposure, starvation, drowning, or disease. The few who made it to foreign lands were rarely welcomed.

Later that week, I visited Grand-Pré. Designated a UNESCO world heritage site, there's almost nothing to distinguish this Nova Scotia farmland area other than an imposing cross commemorating the past and identifying it as having been a prosperous Acadian settlement from 1682 to 1775. The nearby museum does a good job recounting the history of *Le grand dérangement* (The Great Upheaval). It also details the extraordinary way the Acadians built a vibrant community behind the dykes they constructed to hold back the tides, creating acres and acres of fertile land that exist to this day.

On the beautiful afternoon we visited, the surrounding marshlands and meadows were serene and peaceful, the wind gently swayed the tall grass against a backdrop of muddy brown where the recently receded tides now exposed the dyke-lands. Knowing that this was the final deportation site where Acadian families, half of them children, were ordered to leave their homes and forced onto ships, made the moment unbearably mournful and sad. I felt a heaviness in my chest that the serenity of the landscape could not lift.

What the British did was ethnic cleansing. Homeless and running for their lives, the Acadians were *othered* because they had the wrong names, came from the wrong religion, spoke the wrong language—and embodied the wrong potential loyalties.

As a Quebecer, I understand French insecurities about language and culture in a way that many allophones and English speakers in the rest of Canada cannot. I have deep respect for the aspirations of a people who want to preserve and protect what defines them. During that trip, I was proud of my Canadian identity and of everything my parents—and all immigrants—were able to accomplish. But my empathy was not limited to my own Greek ancestors. I was equally disturbed to witness landmarks reminding me of the history of British colonial domination of the French-speaking population in Canada.

Some people have a hard time understanding that multiple loyalties can exist within allophones. They insist we take sides. They are convinced we already have. They say they can tell where our loyalties lie by what language we speak or by our last names.

I can be an allophone Quebecer who supports immigration, believes in the benefits of multiculturalism or even federalism, and also understands and respects francophone efforts for more self-determination and self-preservation. I can support Bill 101 while simultaneously not seeing Montreal's multilingualism as a threat to the survival of French. I can believe in the positive elements of this country, while still calling out Canadian exceptionalism and Quebec bashing. This takes nothing away from my multiple identities or my love and loyalty for my country and province. Just like francophones and anglophones, allophones are not monolithic. To be an allophone in Quebec is to live multiple allegiances. Whether some people see it or even appreciate it, there is a plurality in most Quebecers' lives that is truly a gift.

PART THREE

12. Is There a Magic Formula?

> I believe in integration, not assimilation. I don't
> want to work to become you. I want us to work
> together to create a new whole.
>
> —Hari Kondabolu, American comedian

Immigrants are not a single entity that does X when faced with Y. If you think there is a magic formula or code to crack that will transform an immigrant into a perfectly assimilated Canadian or Quebecer, you'll be disappointed every time. Immigrants, like everyone already here, contain a multitude of values, dreams, and even prejudices. There is no one recipe for an ideal immigration policy, because the ingredients and the dinner guests keep changing.

This notion that we're supposed to bring together hummus, feta, coq au vin, harissa, and bhindi masala and then, by some miraculous government-supported process, transform it into peanut butter and jam—or tourtière—is highly problematic. What's wrong with immigrant groups holding on to their own unique flavours, until we eventually expand the notion of what is considered Canadian or Québécois?

"I almost see chickpeas as an attack on my culture, on who I am," said Quebec columnist Lise Ravary on

French-language radio show *Le club des mal cités* in 2019. "Here, we don't eat chickpeas at 4:00 p.m. in the afternoon coming back from school. That's not who we are."

Ravary was expanding upon one of her *Journal de Montréal* columns where, in an attempt to express her concerns about changes to Canada's new food guide, which had demoted dairy products as a separate food group, she managed to connect "an obsession with chickpeas" as being a "reflection of Canadian multiculturalism."[85]

I was flabbergasted. First off, there's a whole lot of *othering* going on when someone says, "That's not who we are." Who's we? There are plenty of French-speaking kids in Quebec reaching for that hummus without a second thought. How does someone decide what "we" eat or don't eat? Is hummus going to take over and wipe out the cheese curds? Is this the culinary version of the dreaded "Great Replacement," a white-nationalist conspiracy theory that claims that white Europeans are being replaced by non-Europeans through mass migration?

Let's be blunt. If an entire culture is threatened by a legume, maybe it isn't robust enough to survive in the first place.

Homogeneity is not proof of social cohesion or harmony. We do not need to eat the same things, think the same things, or like the same things to ensure social unity. Diversity, whether culinary or social, is not an obstacle or a threat, but an expansion. To expect conformity is to

85 Lise Ravary, "Aimez-vous les pois chiches?" *Journal de Montréal*, January 13, 2019, https://www.journaldemontreal.com/2019/01/13/aimez-vous-les-pois-chiches.

believe—and, in some cases, even legislate—that uniformity is more valuable. It's deeply unrealistic in today's world.

"In the age of mass migration and the internet, cultural plurality is an irreversible fact," writes Indian novelist Salman Rushdie. "Like it or dislike it, it's where we live, and the dream of a pure monoculture is at best an unattainable, nostalgic fantasy and at worst a life-threatening menace."[86]

In Quebec, particularly in the regions, multiculturalism is seen as an existential threat that will bulldoze the province's French language and culture. It is feared that minority ethnic groups will maintain their languages and cultures at the expense of French language and Québécois culture. This view grossly underestimates the importance of francophone culture in Quebec, and the space it takes up, even among allophone and anglophone communities. The fear of disappearance prevents French speakers from seeing how much their culture and language alters *us*.

Not only do most English speakers and allophones speak French in Quebec, they also use French words and expressions even when they're speaking English. There are no patios in Quebec, there are only terrasses. We rarely engage in happy hour, we have a *cinq à sept* or an *apéro*, from the French word apéritif. We don't take the subway, we take the métro. We rent a chalet, rarely a cottage. One does not do an internship here, one does a *stage* (pronounced the French way). Corner stores are always dépanneurs.

---

86 Salman Rushdie, "What This Cultural Debate Needs is More Dirt, Less Pure Stupidity," *The Sunday Times*, December 10, 2005.

No Quebec English speaker or allophone would ever consider poutine or tourtière a Canadian dish, and most of us feel like we've landed in another country when we fly into Calgary or Vancouver. Quebec—where everyone is a minority on one level or another—feels like home to us.

Most importantly, thanks to Bill 101's French-immersion (ironically championed and advocated for not by the Quebec government, but by three English-Quebec moms who wanted their children to be bilingual[87]) and French second-language programs, Quebec's younger anglophones and allophones are the most bilingual and trilingual in the country. Contrary to a popular belief often echoed by Quebec nationalists, Quebec's anglophones are far more bilingual (71 percent) than Quebec francophones (40 percent) when one takes the entire province into consideration. The 2006 census also shows that as many as 80 percent of young anglophones (between fifteen and thirty years of age) are bilingual in Quebec.[88] Unsurprisingly, the majority of bilingual people in Canada have French as their mother tongue.

Most members of Quebec's English-speaking community encourage their children to be bilingual because it increases the odds both of career success and of their remaining here. The English community has lost too

87 "Olga Melikoff, Murielle Parkes and Valerie Neale were leaders of the parent group behind the creation, in 1965, of Canada's first bilingual education program, at Margaret Pendlebury Elementary School in the Montreal suburb of Saint-Lambert, Quebec. Their education activism laid the groundwork for the French immersion system in Canada. As a result of their efforts, Melikoff, Parkes and Neale are often referred to as Canada's 'founding mothers' of French immersion." Kathryn Jezer-Morton, "Canada's 'Founding Mothers' of French immersion," *The Canadian Encyclopedia*, January 9, 2020.

88 Marian Scott, "Census 2016: English is Making Gains in Quebec," *The Gazette*, August 2, 2017.

many of its members to interprovincial migration over the years. Quebec anglophones revel in the opportunity to show off their French, and I've often heard many proudly proclaim that they were told they don't have an accent. Despite what some pundits will tell you, Quebec's anglophones and allophones aren't sick of French; they're sick of the language wars and of being blamed for the perpetual precarity of the French language in the province.

Far from being "backward" or "undemocratic," many immigrants are relieved to have left sectarian and ethnic animosity, misogyny, homophobia, and violence behind. If immigrants were resistant to change, they would have stayed where they were.

In the spring of 2019, I was talking to Beryl, a lively Englishwoman who moved to Quebec over forty years ago. She's part of a group that privately sponsored a Syrian family who had been stuck in a refugee camp in Lebanon. After a few weeks of getting settled in Quebec, Darin, the matriarch of the household, asked if Beryl could take her to get her hair done because "she wanted to feel like a woman again."

Beryl brought her to her own hairdresser in Old Montreal, Bashir, who kissed Darin's hand and asked her how she wanted to be addressed: in French, English, or Arabic. Utterly charmed, Darin later asked Beryl if it would be okay for her to invite him and his wife over for dinner. Beryl said, of course, Bashir and his husband would be delighted by the invite.

"His husband?" Darin wondered whether her grasp of the English language had betrayed her understanding.

"Bashir is gay," Beryl replied. "He has a husband, not a wife."

The Muslim refugee reacted with shock at this news. "This doesn't bother you?" she asked. "Back home, he would be shunned, his lifestyle is not acceptable."

Beryl shrugged and explained that his lifestyle was accepted here, and that being gay simply meant he loved a man, not a woman. Darin continued to mutter that it would not be acceptable back home. Beryl told her that she was under no obligation to see him again, but that things were done differently here. Bashir's choices were not shunned by anyone she knew, and Darin should "just get over it."

Adjusting to a new way of life and a new way of thinking doesn't always take long. Sometimes, you take your cues from your environment. Darin went back to Bashir shortly afterwards, Beryl later informed me. I was not really surprised. Good hairdressers are hard to find.

When analyzing and criticizing the systems in which these *others* were born and raised, it's important to avoid doing two things: first, we should not confuse the political and social systems we disapprove of with the individuals themselves, most of whom fled those very systems to be here. Second, we should not allow white centering to negatively tint our understanding of unfamiliar cultures and societies.

Layla F. Saad addresses this in *Me and White Supremacy*, where she explains that many societies tend to centre whiteness as the norm and everything else as marginal and less important.[89] Political theorist David Moscrop reaches similar conclusions:

> Engaging with diversity doesn't mean giving up your preferences or values declaring 'Well, anything goes!' But what it does require you to accept is that there are other potentially legitimate – if radically different – ways of doing things and attendant sets of preferences that are up for discussion in the public sphere. [...] The converse – digging in and protecting prejudice or ignoring different perspectives because they are unfamiliar – abdicates rational and autonomous politics.[90]

Successful integration requires the receiving majority to see what is benignly different as something that has not become familiar *yet*. That's the magic formula for successful and respectful cohabitation. The same, of course, is required of those who emigrate to a new country. They, too, must change and adjust to the new that will, in turn, shape who they become. This displacement towards something novel encourages a creativity and flexibility that benefits both the immigrant and their new country. Everything new (language, culture, expectations, even the weather) forces a shift in who you are and how you live. Immigration is loss, but it's also a gain. In a way, you're Marie Kondo-ing your life to make room for the new.

---

89 Layla F. Saad, *Me and White Supremacy* (Illinois: Sourcebooks, 2020).

90 David Moscrop, *Too Dumb for Democracy? Why We Make Bad Political Decisions and How We Can Make Better Ones* (Fredericton: Goose Lane Editions, 2019), 215.

13. Parlez-vous avec nous?

The Charter of the French Language, also known as Bill 101, was passed by the National Assembly in 1977. It designates French as the language of the majority and the official language of Quebec. Half a century and seven amendments later, Bill 101 has been instrumental in shaping the Quebec we know today and has ensured that both the French language and francophones' linguistic rights are protected. The goal of the charter was to establish the use of French as the "normal and everyday language of work, instruction, communication, commerce and business," and anyone living and working in today's Quebec would undoubtedly agree that this has overwhelmingly been the result.

Quebec's Quiet Revolution, along with the passing of Bill 101, defined the province and altered its linguistic landscape, enabling the French-speaking majority to take its rightful place as a key player in Quebec's transformation. Even though Bill 101 in effect violated minority-language rights, by sending immigrant children to the French school system, it tackled a very real problem and contributed to the safeguarding of the French language from the ever-present and all-consuming power of English. Over half a century later, while it still rankles some, Bill 101 has been accepted and even lauded for creating new generations of young Quebecers who are perfectly bilingual if not trilingual.

However, since the 1970s, dogmatic policing and overzealousness has been too much a part of everyday life in Quebec. While I respect the spirit of Bill 101, I'm weary of the frequent combativeness and excessively antagonistic attitudes regarding language. You can never protect a language by vilifying another.

Bill 96, An Act Respecting French, the Official and Common language of Québec, which introduces significant and far-reaching amendments to the Charter of the French Language (Bill 101), was adopted on May 24, 2022. It is the most significant overhaul to the Charter since the 1970s and has opened a new can of worms in Quebec and possible new litigation, which, because of the timing of this book's publication, could not be expanded upon.

Quebec's French-language education system has serious long-standing issues. In 2018, the Institut du Québec released a report showing that the province's high-school graduation rate is the lowest in the country, with only 64 percent of public high school students graduating on time.[91] This likely explains why 20 percent of Quebec students attend private schools (most of them highly subsidized), a higher percentage than anywhere else in Canada. In 2008, former Quebec premier Jacques Parizeau wrote an open letter to the English and French school boards, and referred to the situation as

---

91 "Quebec's High School Graduation Rate is Lowest in Canada," *CTV News*, May 2, 2018. English school boards fare better with a 76-percent graduation rate.

"scandalous" and "a tremendous waste that compromises the future."[92]

Fast forward to 2022. Quebec is facing severe teacher shortages—caused by a wave of retirements, poor working conditions, a low starting salary, and overall labour shortages—which have only exacerbated the issue. This is where the government's focus should be. The lack of significant investments in public education can't be remedied by ever more aggressive efforts to eliminate or impede the English language. Whether we like it or not, English has legitimate historical roots in Quebec and throughout Canada.

Although many (particularly those living outside of Montreal) perceive it as such, linguistic insecurity doesn't necessarily mean impending linguistic demise. A recent Angus Reid poll, which found that six in ten Quebecers (63 percent) say they are worried about the future of French in the province, also found that the regions of Quebec most concerned about the future of the French language are those least likely to hear English spoken in their neighbourhoods.[93] This appears to indicate that some of these linguistic insecurities are not based on experience, but rather on fears stoked by pundits and politicians.

It's normal and appropriate to worry about the survival of a minority language. It's not normal to be offended or angered by the presence of other languages in a multicultural city where the majority of its bilingual

---

92   Jacques Parizeau, "Le gâchis scolaire," *Le Journal de Montréal*, September 11, 2008.
93   "Divergent Bilingualism, Linguistic Anxieties, and Bill 96," *Angus Reid Institute*, October 8, 2021.

and trilingual residents have one or two parents born abroad. Montreal serves as a landing pad for almost all of Quebec's new immigrants, not to mention being the province's cosmopolitan business hub; one is bound to hear a lot of English and other languages on the streets of this city.

It's not fair to be angered or exasperated by the fact that French-speaking allophones speak their mother tongues at home or with each other. It's also deeply misleading to use the increasing incidence of languages other than French spoken at home by English speakers and immigrants as proof of the decline of French, as has been done in official statistics and polls—especially when most allophones speak French. Language does not have to be a zero-sum game. Unfortunately, these insecurities are often amplified for political gain or for outrage clicks online by people who think francization should involve linguistic assimilation, not merely successful integration.

Even in the middle of a global pandemic, one of the biggest stories in Quebec in November, 2020, was a *Journal de Montréal* investigative piece about the language spoken by retail clerks in many downtown Montreal stores.[94] "Is the controversial 'bonjour, hi' greeting in downtown Montreal businesses soon to become just 'hi'?" asked the article. "Almost one in two establishments greeted us in English only during a series of hidden-camera tours conducted by our bureau of investigation. Out of 31 shops and restaurants visited in recent weeks, 16 offered a unilingual English greeting."

---

94   Marie-Lise Mormina, "Incapable d'être servi en français," *Le Journal de Montréal*, November 13, 2020.

While an investigation targeting big-box stores in the downtown core amidst a severe labour shortage caused by the pandemic (which often forced businesses to hire unilingual university students) may have skewed results, I do agree that English-only service is not acceptable. Quebec's francophone majority have a right to services in their language, and businesses should be incentivized to provide them. But perhaps the question to ask in a multicultural city like Montreal should always be, "Can francophones be served in their language?" and not, "Are others also being served in theirs?"

This constant vigilance creates conditions where individual citizens feel completely comfortable accosting a stranger on Twitter for communicating in English (as if Bill 101 regulates people's social media accounts), and allows the Office québécois de la langue française (OQLF) to be hijacked for political purposes. The organization's mandate is to protect and promote the French language. This includes defining official terminology, monitoring the status of French in the province, and helping business owners navigate language laws. There is nothing inherently political or partisan about the OQLF (which was created by the Liberals, a federalist party, after all) and it has an important job to do.

But the extreme antipathy many Quebecers have for English and the way it's depicted as the language of colonization and oppression (which it was for so very long) leads to overzealousness in language protection. This is how we make international headlines when language inspectors fine businesses over bizarre transgressions.

In 2016, a pub owner was warned by the OQLF that a small coaster-sized TripAdvisor sticker on his storefront window could be contravening language laws.[95] The owner of famous Montreal restaurant Joe Beef complained that inspectors took issue with an antique sign above the staff bathroom that says "please leave this gate closed."[96] Another owner received warnings about the word *caffè*.[97] OQLF visits were particularly unwelcome during the pandemic, when restaurants were struggling to stay alive. One franchise owner, who had trademarked his business name and had already settled a complaint with the OQLF back in 2013, was irate to see language inspectors show up at his place again.[98]

No story summarizes the absurdity of it all more than Pastagate, which managed to put Quebec on the map for all the wrong reasons. In 2013, the OQLF tried to get upscale Italian restaurant Buonanotte to replace the words pasta, calamari, and antipasto on its menu with French terms. Not only did the incident lead to a barrage of jokes and international headlines mocking the government agency, it led to the resignation of Louise Marchand, then-president of the OQLF, and forced the agency to modernize its approach to language complaints.[99]

Pastagate was so comical, it prompted satirical magazine *The Beaverton* to invent a story about Bouton,

95   "OQLF Warns Burgundy Lion Pub that TripAdvisor Window Sticker Could Violate Language Laws," *The Gazette*, January 29, 2016.
96   Benjamin Shingler, "Top Montreal Restaurant Yet Another Victim of 'Overzealous Language Inspectors,'" *Toronto Star*, February 23, 2013.
97   "Italian Coffee Shop in Montreal in Trouble with Language Watchdog," *CBC News*, March 2, 2013.
98   Felicia Parrillo, "Visit from Language Watchdog Leaves Montreal Restaurant Owner Furious," *Global News*, October 23, 2020.
99   Dan Delmar, "The OQLF has a Problem with 'Pasta' (Pastagate)," *CJAD*, February 19, 2013.

an English-speaking parrot at the Montreal Biodome that was being deported to Toronto following a surprise visit to the zoo by Florence Laplante, Chief of Animal Compliance at the Office québécois de la langue française: "On both occasions, Bouton only spoke to visitors in English," Laplante complained. "She asked for crackers, not *craquelins*."[100]

Even more surreal was that many Quebecers thought *The Beaverton* story was a real news report. Incidents like these do absolutely nothing for the protection and promotion of the French language. They only succeed in making us look parochial and paranoid.

And yet, francophones are correct when they claim that some members of Quebec's English community have a long-standing disinterest in—and sometimes even antipathy towards ––francophone culture, often propelled by their fear of separatist politics, and want little to do with their francophone neighbours. In 2021, *Gazette* columnist Lise Ravary, commenting on Quebec's English-speaking community overlooking the passing of beloved Québécois singer Michel Louvain, wrote, "Why are so many of us skittish about crossing the culture divide, considering we already share a home?"[101] Almost fifty years after Bill 101 came into existence, some of the province's "angryphones" are still around, threatening to leave rather than make the effort to learn French.

"All these [older] people are stuck in the past, fighting old battles," Noah Sidel, a young father of three, told me

---

100 "Parrot Removed from Montreal Biodome after Learning Too Much English," *The Beaverton*. July 12, 2013.

101 Lise Ravary, "Francophones Mourn Michel Louvain, Anglos Say 'Who?" *The Gazette*, April 19, 2021.

when we spoke in 2020. "We actually benefited the most from Bill 101. Some folks are still fighting on the Plains of Abraham. Post-Bill 101 francophone kids are much more secure in their linguistic identity because their parents already won the battle. They can be open to new cultures because they feel secure in their own identity."[102]

Sidel believes in the pragmatic aspect of learning French. "If you don't look at the issue emotionally, why would anyone living here refuse to learn French? Bill 101 works. It made Quebec much stronger, allowed us to become much more rooted in our society here and forced an older generation to come to terms with that."

A quick glance at Statistics Canada figures corroborates Sidel's point. Of English-speaking Quebecers, 71 percent are bilingual, up from 68 percent in 2011. That number jumps to 80 percent between the ages of 18 and 34. An impressive 94.4 percent of Quebecers of all linguistic backgrounds are able to have a conversation in French, to get by, *se débrouiller*, as we say in good Québécois, making Quebec our most bilingual province and Montreal our most trilingual city.[103]

Unlike in the 1960s, when immigrants—even French-speakers if they were not Catholic—were sent to the English-run Protestant school system, Bill 101 ensures francization. New immigrants have no choice but to educate their children in French. As a result, allophones are increasingly speaking French as their first official language.

---

102 Toula Drimonis, "What if Quebec's Anglophones Aren't the Problem Some Think They Are?" *Cult MTL*, December 10, 2020.

103 "Linguistic Characteristics of Canadians," *Statistics Canada*, July 23, 2018.

"A majority of new immigrants in every census since 1971 have chosen French more often than English as their adopted language. Statistics Canada's 2011 National Household Survey of Canada reported that for the first time in modern history, the first official language of more than half of Quebec immigrants was French."[104]

While recent focus has been on the decline of the French language in Montreal, critics argue that this is due to francophones moving to the suburbs, skewing Montreal's numbers because it is a landing pad for immigrants. Another extremely questionable element of this debate is that the rise of mother tongues other than French is used as proof of the decline of French. But English as a mother tongue has also been declining. The reason is simple. With demographics shifting both in Quebec and across Canada, there are now more people whose first language is neither English nor French. You know, allophones like me. The latest StatCan data projects that by 2031, allophones will comprise around 29 to 32 percent of the total Canadian population.

What's equally important to understand is that allophones are often counted in a census by (a) their mother tongue and (b) the language spoken most often at home. But they will also declare their mother tongue, a third language, on an equal footing with French or English.

Laval University sociology professor and former head of the language statistics program at Statistics Canada, Jean-Pierre Corbeil's research concludes that determining language identity by these two measurements is no longer sufficient or accurate because in complex

---

104 Marian Scott, "French Gains Ground Among Newcomers," *The Gazette*, May 9, 2013.

linguistic environments such as Quebec, languages overlap and multilingualism exists.

Corbeil writes, "The Quebec environment, and in particular Montreal, is multilingual, but it is a multilingualism that does not produce English unilingualism."[105]

Corbeil says that he has an increasingly hard time with categorizing people as "allophones," "francophones" or "anglophones", because these concepts are often reductionist and linguistic practices are increasingly fluid in Quebec.

When Air Canada CEO Michael Rousseau, giving an English-only speech at the Montreal Chamber of Commerce in the fall of 2021, admitted to not understanding French despite living here for the past fourteen years, he managed to unite Quebecers of all linguistic backgrounds in outrage. Rousseau's tone-deaf assertion that not needing to speak French in Montreal was a "testament to the city" threatened to undo years of hard-earned linguistic peace. His comment immediately harkened back to the "Speak White" era, when anglophone bosses refused to speak French with their employees, and opened the door for hardliners to once again demand limits to the use of English language.

Anglophones were livid that francophones would think he was representative of them. The Quebec Community Groups Network, representing English-language organizations across the province, quickly issued a statement: "Mr. Rousseau's narrow-minded comment that he does not feel the need to learn French feeds the myth that English-speaking Quebecers are a

---

105 Jean-Benoît Nadeau, « Pour en finir avec le déclin de la langue française », L'Actualité, April 9, 2022.

privileged minority indifferent to French." Among politicians loudly demanding action were Liberal MNA Marwah Rizqy and Québec Solidaire MNA Ruba Ghazal, both from allophone, immigrant families. Their outcry prompted columnist Antoine Robitaille to call them "inspiring" and TV producer Michel Trudeau to tweet: "It took the CEO of Air Canada to better understand that the future of French in America now passes through people called Rizqy and Ghazal." The politicians' reactions were neither inspiring nor surprising to me. What I continue to find surprising is that some francophones stubbornly refuse to believe that non-francophones want to protect French too.

The biggest irony is that immigration is not and never has been a threat to the majority language. Rather, with birth rates plummeting and the older generation dying, immigration is exactly how it will continue thriving. In September of 2020, Ruba Ghazal wrote an op-ed expressing her love for the French language as a child of Bill 101.

"I was ten years old when I arrived in Quebec," she wrote in *Le Soleil*. "I didn't speak French. Thirty-two years later, Quebec and French form part of my identity as important as my [cultural] origins."[106]

Former PQ party leader Jean-François Lisée immediately tweeted the article, adding: "The only thing missing from this excellent letter is THE most important measure for the future: a knowledge of French as a prerequisite for immigrating to Quebec (except for refugees).

---

106 Ruba Ghazal, "Lettre d'une enfant de la loi 101," *Le Soleil*, September 21, 2020.

Everything else has less of an impact. Therefore, let's make more of an effort!"

Without skipping a beat, Ghazal tweeted back. "If your measures were in place the year I arrived in Quebec, my parents and I would have not been able to immigrate here and I would have not had the pleasure of responding to your tweet."

The exchange, of course, took place in impeccable French.

Every new immigrant who arrives here is required to learn French. And if they don't speak it as adequately as some people would want them to, I guarantee you their kids will—and with a Québécois accent so gloriously thick their parents will wonder who they are. Just ride the Montreal metro when school is letting out and tell me I'm wrong.

Take a look at a list of 2019 Montreal finalists for *La Dictée*. An annual French spelling bee of sorts, it's a way for Quebec students to improve and master their use of French while learning about the world around them. Out of the fifteen finalists, maybe three were what purists would call *de souche* (old stock) Quebecers. I scanned the other names and saw Vishwa Narayanswamy, Pearl Wang, Vyke Ajemian, Ismael Girard, Celina Chang, Fairoz Aly. Not only were these first- or second-generation immigrant children not endangering the French language, they were *excelling* in it. *They* will pass it down to their kids, ensuring the language survives on this continent.

In spite of what politicians and pundits assert, French isn't threatened by a store clerk uttering "Bonjour, hi!" in downtown Montreal, or by a trilingual allophone tweeting in English. It's threatened when it's not taught properly, not used accurately, and when a population isn't enticed by it. "What you love eventually survives," says a Senegalese proverb. "Love is a verb," said bell hooks. The onus shouldn't always be on everyone else. You can't guilt someone into speaking a language, or slap their wrists every time they don't. But you can make it easier for them to learn it, you can make them fall in love with it, you can make it cool to speak it, and you can encourage people to revel in its nuances and its wonderfully distinctive joual.[107]

I adore living in a multicultural, polyglot city like Montreal; I love that the city's heart and soul remains unquestionably French. And I expect French to remain Quebec's official and common language, if for no other reason than this is what distinguishes us from the rest of North America.

Quebec French is uniquely Québécois. It is a language that gives a voice to a population that may have ties to colonial France, but has evolved into its own distinct group on a continent surrounded by English. Quebec French, and all French dialects across Canada, speak to the challenges, the hopes and the dreams of a people. And yet, so often it's treated as a substandard, folkloric version of French, even by the very people who speak it. In the preface of her book, *La langue rapaillée*, which addresses Quebec's linguistic insecurity, linguist

---

107 *Joual* is associated with the French-speaking working class in Montreal and is often looked down upon. It has historically been a source of insecurity and shame for Quebecers. It is only in recent years that it has become something to celebrate.

Anne-Marie Beaudoin-Bégin offers a moving homage to Quebec French.

> *Qu'est-ce que le français québécois? C'est la langue des marins, la langue des habitants, la langue des Filles du Roy, la langue des ecclésiastiques, la langue des coureurs des bois, la langue des aristocrates, aussi. Le français québécois, c'est la langue de la persistance, la langue des longs hivers, la langue des veillées, la langue des grosses familles. C'est la langue de la Revanche des berceaux et de la Révolution tranquille.*[108]

> What is Quebec French? It's the language of sailors, the language of its inhabitants [settlers], the language of the 'King's Daughters,' the language of clergymen, the language of fur traders, the language of aristocrats, too. Quebec French is the language of persistence, of long winters, of evening gatherings, the language of large families. It's the language of the Revenge of the Cradle and of the Quiet Revolution.

It's uniquely Quebec. What else could it possibly be? Just reading Beaudoin-Bégin's homage to the particularities of this language is enough to move me, because I recognize and love all the references as my own. Quebec French to me is hearing Céline Dion singing Luc Plamondon's "L'amour existe encore" and Les BB with "Donne-moi ma chance" when I was first learning the language. It's Corneille, Félix Leclerc, and Cœur

---

108 Anne-Marie Beaudoin-Bégin, *La Langue Rapaillée: Combattre l'Insécurité Linguistique des Québécois.* (Montreal: Éditions Somme toute, 2015).

de pirate in my ears. It's "*Prochain arrêt, Berri-UQAM*" and almost certainly "*Interruption de service prolongée ligne orange…*" while riding the metro. It's the words of Michel Tremblay and Fanny Britt, *La Presse* and Radio-Canada, the Théâtre La Chapelle and the comedy of Marc Labrèche.

It's Jean-Marc-Vallée's *C.R.A.Z.Y.* and Sunday nights with Guy A. Lepage on *Tout le monde en parle*. It's shouting "*Aweille*" and "Lâche pas la patate!" and "Voyons donc!" and saying depanneur and guichet instead of corner store and bank machine. It's knowing what the acronyms BANQ and SPVM stand for, and the crucial difference between the SAQ and the SAAQ. It's the language that defines my home and my days. It's "*Mesdames et messieurs, bienvenue à Montréal*" when the plane lands and we're finally home.

I wish Quebec francophones understood how much this language they love is loved by us, too.

14. The Burden of Majority Bias

By 2016, in the wake of the US financial crisis of 2007-8 that rippled around the world, Greece had plunged into the worst economic crisis the country had ever seen. As a result of structural weaknesses, loss of revenues due to chronic tax evasion, and a bloated and underperforming public infrastructure, the country was buried in insurmountable debt. The lack of monetary policy flexibility on the part of the Eurozone did not help matters.

Desperately needed financial aid came at a very high price—too high, some have argued. A series of reforms and austerity measures imposed by the International Monetary Fund led to a full-blown humanitarian crisis that exacted a terrible human cost. "Economic depression, slashed pensions, tragic suicides borne out of desperation, abysmal unemployment rates, and a worrisome brain drain, were just some of the tragic results."[109]

On April 6th of that year, I was reading a *La Presse* article, "'Influenceurs': les défis de représenter la société" ("'Influencers': the challenge of representing society"), about some individuals in Quebec media who toil behind the scenes as producers, editors-in-chief, and TV and radio researchers. Even if the general public doesn't necessarily know who they are, they play a huge role in

---

109 Toula Drimonis, "The Terrible Price Greece Continues to Pay," *Ricochet*, September 8, 2018.

shaping the news. They are the gatekeepers who decide who to invite to popular talk shows, whom to interview, whose opinions and expertise is disseminated, and what angles are broached.

Scrolling down through the *La Presse* piece, I was increasingly uncomfortable with the uninterrupted list of white francophones. Although Montreal is culturally diverse, Quebec media and public institutions are not. Quebec French-language TV routinely hosts all-white panels responding to questions like: "Is systemic racism real?" or "Does racial profiling exist?" By that logic, I expect an all-male panel discussing menstrual cramps to appear on my TV any day now.

Similarly, in the summer of 2020, a *Journal de Montréal* series of articles on how Quebec entrepreneurs would tackle the COVID crisis featured almost no racial or gender diversity.[110] All eight entrepreneurs profiled on the front page were white and male. And this, while immigrants and members of marginalized ethnic groups routinely top the ranks of Quebec's self-employed and are usually found to have higher business ownership rates than the native-born population.[111] How was it that not a single editor looked at that front page and recognized that it didn't reflect today's Quebec?

I can appreciate the journalistic grind of hustling to find people when your resources and time are limited, and how convenient it is to reach for experts you know.

---

110 "Le Québec Inc. se réinvente," *Journal de Montréal*, June 6, 2020.

111 Garnett Picot, Yuri Ostrovsky, "Immigrant and Second-Generation Entrepreneurs in Canada: An Intergenerational Comparison of Business Ownership," *Statistics Canada*, September 22, 2021, https://www150.statcan.gc.ca/n1/pub/36-28-0001/2021009/article/00003-eng.htm.

But then I came across a paragraph in the article that left me aggravated beyond words.

Charles-Alexandre Théorêt, a researcher for popular TV show, *La soirée est (encore) jeune* and a former casting director for *125, Marie-Anne*, had this to say when asked about the lack of cultural diversity on French-language shows: "These cultural communities aren't there because their members don't always speak French. The number of times that I've searched for Greeks to speak to me about the political situation in Greece… They all speak English! I can't put them on the air."

Imagine my surprise reading his quote *in French* … only to find out that, as a Greek Quebecer, I really couldn't. My knowledge of French is good enough that it has afforded me the joy of working in that language, including on air in the broadcast media. I know plenty of Montreal Greeks who speak French perfectly. Lawyers, doctors, professors, a bunch of fifteen-year-olds, you name it, I know them. A simple request on social media would have netted what he needed very quickly and with very little effort.

Moreover, there was someone close by who was ideally suited for this conversation. Someone whose office should have been contacted immediately, but wasn't. The general consul of Greece at the Montreal Consulate at the time was a man by the name of Nicolas Sigalas. He is now at the Greek Consulate in Beijing, China, but at the height of the crisis, Sigalas was working and living in Montreal. Not only does he speak French, it is his first language, having been born and raised in Brussels. Here was a man ideally suited to speak on the subject matter but who was never given the chance.

Théorêt's assumption was that members of the Greek community in Montreal don't speak French. Perhaps this was his conclusion after interacting with pre-Bill-101 Montreal Greeks who hadn't been educated in French adequately, or perhaps he was told something along those lines by someone else. Either way, he believed in the story of unilingual anglophone Greeks so strongly he never even thought to see for himself whether it was true.

More than fifty years after Bill 101 came into effect, many francophone Quebecers still think that Quebec's allophones either can't or won't speak French. The lack of ethnic diversity in French-language media continues to lag behind English media.[112] It's a loss for Quebecers. They are not getting the full story.

No one writes about the dangers of an incomplete story better than Nigerian author Chimamanda Adichie. In the author's TED Talk, she describes the shock of her American roommate when she went to the US for university.

"She asked where I had learned to speak English so well and was confused when I explained that Nigeria happened to have English as its official language. She asked if she could listen to what she called my 'tribal' music and was consequently very disappointed when I produced my tape of Mariah Carey. She assumed that I did not know how to use a stove. What struck me was this… she had felt sorry for me even before she saw me, her default position towards me as an African was a kind of patronizing well-meaning pity. My roommate had a single story

---

112 Étienne Paré, "Les médias anglophones plus représentatifs de diversité que ceux du Québec," *Le Devoir*, November 26, 2021.

of Africa. A single story of catastrophe. In this single story, there was no possibility of Africans being like her, in any way. No possibility of feelings more complex than pity, no possibility of a connection as human equals.[113]

Adichie goes on to share a criticism leveled against her by a professor who thought her novel wasn't "authentically African" because her characters were "too much like him, an educated and middle-class man." They "drove cars, they were not starving, therefore they were not authentically African."

Adichie explains that "the single story creates stereotypes, and the problem with stereotypes is not that they are untrue, but that they are incomplete. They make one story become the only story."

If you've heard that all Italians are part of the mob, all Greeks work in restaurants, all Haitians are in gangs, all French Canadians are on welfare, and all English live in Westmount or the West Island and refuse to speak French, then you've come across generalizations and clichés. Unconscious bias about minorities is a dangerous thing when mainstream media has a way of both reflecting and propagating these stereotypes. We see this play out often in Quebec, with mainstream media portraying communities using outdated or inaccurate images and racist tropes, or by choosing to report the news from a white-centric point of view.

"No one is impartial," I wrote in an editorial for the *Fédération professionnelle des journalistes du Québec*'s magazine, *Le Trente*. Further,

---

113 Chimamanda Ngozi Adichie, "The Danger of a Single Story," *TED Talks*, October 7, 2009, https://www.youtube.com/watch?v=D9Ihs241zeg&vl=en.

This long-vaunted notion of journalistic objectivity is a lie and mainstream journalism is often guilty of mirroring, perpetuating, and refusing to challenge mainstream majority bias. We all come to the table with our own background, perspectives, and limitations shaped by our unique lifepath. There is no such thing as a 'view from nowhere,' as philosopher Thomas Nagel argues. If we want balanced, inclusive, and informed reporting, we can no longer afford to underestimate how unconscious bias works and how many subjective decisions lead to *what* and *who* makes the news.[114]

In March 2020, the *Journal de Montréal* published an article on street gangs and someone on staff decided to run an archived picture of what they assumed was a street gang—a group of Black youth. Turns out, the image they chose depicted Black students from Calixa-Lavallée high school waiting in line to enter—of all things—a church in Montreal North. The nine minors and their parents are now suing the *Journal* and publisher Québecor for defamation.[115]

An example of Islamophobia in Quebec mainstream media occurred when the *Journal de Québec* published an article in 2016 with the headline: "Thousands of lambs slaughtered for a Muslim festival." The fact that Quebecers annually slaughter countless turkeys and pigs for Christmas and Thanksgiving was irrelevant and clearly "not the same" for the author of this piece, or its intended audience.

114 Toula Drimonis, "More Diversity in Media Means More Accurate Reporting," *Le Trente* 44 (Fall 2020).
115 Naomie Gelper, "*Le Journal de Montréal* poursuivi pour une photo fausse et stigmatisante envers les Noirs," *Métro*, June 30, 2021.

"You're a vegetarian or a vegan and are outraged by this story, and feel slightly ill? You have a right to be," I wrote in response to the article. "But if you're a meat-eating Quebecer and you're feigning outrage at a story about other meat-eating Quebecers, what exactly are you upset about? Is it that they're killing animals and/or eating meat while being practising Muslims?"[116]

A few years later the *Journal de Montréal* followed suit, proclaiming with alarm that "All Quebecers are eating halal."[117] It was grab-your-kids-and-save-yourselves sensationalistic stuff, published with the intent to shock. I routinely pick up halal and kosher products when I shop. The notion that halal is somehow barbaric, dirty, uncivilized, or even headline-worthy is nothing more than Islamophobia.

Speaking of kosher, a popular anti-Semitic conspiracy theory claims the kosher certification found on food is a "kosher tax" collected to finance Jewish and more specifically Zionist organizations engaged in religious wars. During the 2014 Quebec provincial elections, PQ candidate Louise Mailloux, while defending the need for a Quebec Charter of Values, revived those claims. When Canadian Jewish advocacy organizations called on Mailloux to debunk the dangerous falsehoods, she apologized but did not retract her statement. Quebec Premier Pauline Marois defended her candidate as a respected academic. "Her writings are eloquent. I respect

---

116 Toula Drimonis, "Newspaper Report Shameful and Bigoted Finger Pointing at Muslim Traditions," *Daily Hive*, September 13, 2016.
117 Geneviève Lajoie, "Tous les Québécois mangent Halal, " *Le Journal de Montréal*, March 14, 2012.

her point of view. She supports our secular charter and I appreciate her support."[118]

When unconscious bias is pointed out, the reaction is often denial and deflection. The accusation of "identity politics" is used to brand valid criticism by minorities as exaggerated whining or a calculated attack on the majority.

After a number of articles had been written imploring the Quebec government to push forward the motion to regulate the status of asylum seekers working on the COVID frontlines, *Journal de Montréal* columnist Richard Martineau wrote a piece titled "*Prison identaire*" (Identity Prison). In it, he deplored the fact that the focus seemed to be on Haitian women working in healthcare, as if thousands of other ethnic groups weren't also working in the field. He writes,

> Do you know what they all have in common? They're Quebecers. Not Italian Quebecers or Irish Quebecers. Not transgender Quebecers or non-binary red-headed Quebecers who believe in Allah, Jesus, or Elvis Presley. Quebecers who live here, in Quebec.
>
> These people aren't immigrants who live in Quebec. They're citizens, full-fledged Quebecers. Let's stop wanting to tie them to their country of origin. It's not a favour to them. Or to us. Real anti-racism, the real kind, is to not care where

118 Les Perreaux, "Marois Defends PQ Candidate Accused of Anti-Semitic Beliefs," *The Globe and Mail*, March 14, 2014.

people come from. And to attach no importance to the colour of their skin.[119]

A lovely sentiment, just like the evergreen "I don't see colour." Aside from the irony of having a columnist who makes his name denigrating ethnic and religious minorities pretend that he's above racism, there's a total lack of appreciation for complexity. How could he claim that these people are full-fledged Quebecers when they live in a precarious state of uncertainty and are not entitled to the same benefits as others? Their immigration applications were still waiting to be assessed while they performed dangerous and backbreaking work that most Quebecers wouldn't do. How are they the *same* when they are being treated *differently*?

When Martineau and others accuse minority groups of engaging in "identity politics" and being "confined to an identity prison" he fails to understand how people can be composed of multiple identities, and that the majority often reacts negatively to these identities. It might be easy for a white francophone man with a popular column in Quebec's most-read French-language newspaper to say he doesn't see colour and doesn't care where you're from, but clearly he does.

You can't tell people not to focus on parts of their identity that have given them grief. People *do* see colour and *do* see religion and *do* see gender. Pretending otherwise because none of these systemic injustices ever affect *you* isn't freedom from identity prison, it's denial. The goal should be to eradicate *bias* against these differences, not eradicate the differences themselves.

119 Richard Martineau, "Prison identitaire," *Le Journal de Montréal*, May 19, 2020.

15. Quebec Nationalism: All or Nothing?

> Nationalism is an infantile thing.
> It is the measles of mankind.
> —Albert Einstein

I'm proud of being Greek. I love our history and what we have contributed to civilization. I appreciate our culture, our cuisine, our gorgeous landscapes. I rejoice in how warm and inviting Greeks can be. I think they're special.

But, at the risk of offending some members of the Greek community who might feel otherwise, I don't think they're more special than anyone else. I don't think Greek history deserves to be preserved at the expense of other histories. I don't retain my language and culture out of patriotic duty. I do it out of love.

If someone were to tell me that, down the line, Greeks decided it was too much effort and they let the language and history die out, I'd find it unfortunate and it would sadden me. But I'd also just shrug and say, "Well... we had a good run."

It was comedian Doug Stanhope who said that nationalism "teaches you to take pride in shit you haven't done and hate people you've never met." George Carlin said, "Being Irish isn't a skill. It's a fucking genetic accident.

You wouldn't say, I'm proud to be five eleven. Proud to have a predisposition to have colon cancer. Why the fuck would you be proud to be Irish?" He referred to excessive national pride and exceptionalism as "delusional thinking."

Nationalism is tribal, inward-looking, and self-centred. American writer and activist Bryant H. McGill refers to it as "a form of collective narcissism." It demands that we close ourselves off to everything and everyone that doesn't fit into our manufactured national identity.

Of course, I'm not referring to the mostly harmless patriotism that makes us get emotional over our national anthems, or flag waving during the Olympic Games. That reaction, too, is nothing more than conditioning, but it's at least not dangerous. It's the other kind that I'm leery of. The kind that seeks to elevate *us* at the cost of *them*. Reactionary nationalism is at the very root of everything that is ugly about attempts to control, limit, or completely stall immigration. It talks as if hordes of invaders will burn everything that you love to the ground.

"*The barbarians at the gate*," as Greek poet Constantine P. Cavafy wrote.[120] The danger from outside that threatens everything within, as war-mongering leaders and far-right pundits try to convince us. Because, asks Cavafy, *without them, who are we?*

> *Now what's going to happen to us without barbarians?*

---

120 Constantine P. Cavafy, *Waiting for the Barbarians, Collected Poems*, trans. Edmund Keeley and Philip Sherrard (Princeton: Princeton University Press,1975).

Those people were a kind of solution.

Without an external threat, Cavafy says, some people are unable to rally together. If that threatening force doesn't exist, then we must manufacture one.

Quebec historian Jean-Francois Nadeau described this kind of anti-immigrant nationalism in *Le Devoir*: "To hear them, the maintenance of an identity would be conditional on a permanent confrontation against a willingly fabricated enemy: the Stranger, the Other."[121]

He accused those who insist that the preservation of a national identity supersedes everything, and who see immigrants as a perpetual enemy, of "curling up forever in the illusion of their permanence." Concluding that "such speech does not invent anything," he recognized that it's the same old recycled xenophobia and racism.

As demographics in Quebec continue to change, and the proportion of francophones and anglophones continues to decrease while the allophone population increases, we are witnessing the emergence of an ethno-nationalist panic that veers considerably to the right. A rigid, conservative, angry nationalism that isn't inclusive or welcoming but is deeply xenophobic, treating immigrants as colossal obstacles to French Quebec's survival. It's why many *independantistes* have subsequently removed themselves from the movement, not wanting to associate with this newfound toxic nationalism.

This attitude has created a major conundrum for ethno-nationalists and the politicians who pander to them: while they're intent on radically reducing immigration

---

121 Jean-François Nadeau, "Les identités passagères," *Le Devoir*, November 1, 2021.

because it supposedly threatens the French character of Quebec, they still need to find solutions to the problems of an aging population and a low birth rate.

Brexit was driven by fear of migrants, as was Donald Trump's electoral win. Quebec's CAQ government was largely elected in 2019 on a promise to reduce immigration by 20 percent, with Premier Legault famously proclaiming, *"En prendre moins, mais en prendre soin."* We will take fewer, but care for them better. Fewer, despite the province suffering from labour shortages in all regions, and business groups pleading for an *increase* in immigration.[122]

Two years later, faced with chronic labour shortages and a pandemic that significantly reduced immigration, the Legault government was forced to backtrack and raise quotas.[123] Ideology can't compete with reality. But it can temporarily solicit extra votes.

Fear of newcomers is almost always driven by misinformation. Ask people wary of migrants, and you will see how exaggerated the menace appears. People who harbour anti-immigrant sentiments tend to believe the number of immigrants living in their country is higher than it actually is, and that immigrants are taking more than they're giving. Even people who don't have strong opinions on the subject can be swayed by misleading and sensationalist headlines. These days, the brunt of xenophobia is felt by the Muslim community.

---

122 Giuseppe Valiante, "Quebec Has Accepted 40 percent Skilled Workers in First Half of 2019," *The Canadian Press*, August 23, 2019.

123 "Quebec Will Raise Immigration Quotas, Minister Confirms," *The Canadian Press*, April 22, 2021.

In 2015, the *Economist* found that Europeans "wildly overestimate the proportion of their populations that is Muslim: an Ipsos-Mori poll found that on average French respondents thought 31 percent of their compatriots were Muslim, against an actual figure closer to 8 percent."[124]

Canadians don't fare much better. A 2015 survey conducted by Ipsos Reid revealed that the average Canadian estimates that Muslims form 20 percent of the country's population. The actual figure is 3.2 percent. "The gap between actual Muslim Canadians and those who exist only in the public imagination is over 5.5 million people—roughly equal the population of Toronto. Fears of Islam's demographic triumph are greatly exaggerated."[125]

The average Quebecer is no different, thinking the figure to be above 17 percent when it's actually 3.1 percent. Who can blame them when the province's most popular newspaper persists in their unhealthy obsession and repeatedly portrays Muslims in a negative light? A 2016 National Council of Canadian Muslims youth workshop in Montreal exploring Islamophobia in the media found that 94 percent of participants said they felt media portrayals of Muslims in Quebec were negative. It's no surprise that legislation like the PQ's proposed Charter of Values or the CAQ's Bill 21 (Quebec legislation that prohibits the wearing of religious symbols such as hijabs, kippas and turbans by teachers and other government employees deemed to be in positions of authority) has been met with popular support. Support

124 "Islam in Europe," *The Economist*, January 7, 2015.
125 Deane McRobie, "Canada's Imaginary Muslims," *iPolitics*, January 19, 2015, https://ipolitics.ca/2015/01/19/canadas-imaginary-muslims.

for these political reforms comes from lawmakers and pundits exaggerating the "problem" by portraying "others" as demanding more concessions to the detriment of the majority. Then they amplify that problem by making the group larger than it actually is. The end result is a majority concluding that we are being "invaded" by hordes of *others*.

It's fascinating to see the fear of and misconceptions about immigrants or members of religious minorities even in a country like Canada, which welcomes over three hundred thousand newcomers a year—one of the highest rates per population of any country in the world.

"Immigrants account for almost a quarter of Canada's labour force, and up to 90% of its labour force growth," writes Andray Domise in *Maclean's*. "Without immigration, the Conference Board of Canada projects that deaths in this country would exceed births by the year 2034, that the labour force would shrink, social services would face 'significant difficulties' in funding, and the necessary tax hikes would likely cause businesses to forego investment in this country (if not pull up stakes and leave)."[126]

Canada not only depends upon immigration, it does extremely well *because* of it, routinely ranking at or near the top of the annual Quality of Life Index.[127] Political stability, accessible healthcare, civil safety, and a high standard of living were just some of the criteria measured in the global-rankings system. As Canadians, we live our

126 Andray Domise, "The Rise of an Uncaring Canada," *Maclean's*, April 21, 2019.
127 "Canada is the No. 1 Country in the World, According to the 2021 Best Countries Report," *Yahoo Finance*, April 13, 2021, https://ca.style. yahoo.com/canada-no-1-country-world-040100737.html.

lives surrounded by people who come from somewhere else. I don't know how anyone can look around and not see that they make this country better.

Ethnic nationalism will often first emerge subtly, as politicians and pundits test the waters. Politicians like Donald Trump in the US, Marine Le Pen and Éric Zemmour in France, and Viktor Orbán in Hungary used coded language. It's not about racism or xenophobia, they explain, they just don't fit in here, they have "different values." In 2017, when Canadian Conservative Party candidate Kelly Leitch pledged to redraft Canada's immigration policy, the cornerstone of her plan was for each new immigrant to be screened for "anti-Canadian values."[128]

"Do they support the ideas of hard work, generosity, freedom and tolerance? Do they believe men and women are equal?" were some of the questions Leitch asked in a campaign video. Similar to when the Conservative Party attempted to create a "barbaric cultural practices" hotline in 2015, Leitch explained that she just wanted to make sure Canada received the "right kind" of newcomers. In the end, Leitch's proposal to concretize Canadian values by demonizing Muslims and minorities failed spectacularly and was widely ridiculed. It turned out to be a litmus test for a very real Canadian value: an unwillingness to fall for immigrant *othering*.

Quebec has had its own brushes with attempting to define the "right kind" of immigrant. In 2007, the small

---

128 Kellie Leitch, "Kellie Leitch on Screening for Canadian Values," Kellie Leitch for Leader of the Conservative Party, February 25, 2017, campaign video, https://www.youtube.com/watch?v=o_ tApV8fTrc&t=196s.

town of Hérouxville adopted a code of conduct to "help-fully" remind new arrivals that women do not hide their faces in Quebec, are allowed to drive cars, and can write cheques. Particularly, they were not to be burned alive or murdered in honour killings, implying this is a significant problem among immigrants. It was moot to the Hérouxville lawmakers that Canadian and Quebec laws against discrimination, domestic violence, and murder already exist, and that Quebec women are vulnerable to domestic violence no matter their ethnic origins. The code went on, inexplicably, to clarify the importance of Christmas trees, as if swarms of jihadis were descending on rural Quebec to personally make sure *ma tante Odette* would never again decorate her house in preparation for *Papa Noël*.

Hérouxville is a small rural farming parish near Mauricie, Quebec, with a population of fewer than fourteen hundred residents. They are likely all white, Roman Catholic, and francophone. The town council decided to compile this code of behaviour despite the fact that no immigrants live there. It was devised as a precaution, a warning, and, most definitely, a deterrent.

A deterrent, the way Laurentian towns like St. Faustin and Ste. Agathe used to have *Jews Keep Out* signs in the 1930s and 40s, and the way Ontario's cottage country was littered with *Christians Only* and *Only to Approved Gentiles* notices in the 50s. The Hérouxville townsfolk weren't explicitly saying *No Muslims,* but they were ready to stop them from even thinking of living there.

The code, as exaggerated and groan-worthy as it might appear to most of us, didn't materialize out of thin air. At the time, the debate on "reasonable accommodations"[129] was raging in Quebec (the phrase arising from the Bouchard-Taylor Commission, officially the Quebec Consultation Commission on Accommodation Practices Related to Cultural Differences). It led many in "the regions" (that is, outside Montreal), often with no first-person knowledge of immigrants, to assume that French Quebecers were bending over backwards to accommodate newcomers and religious extremists.

Pay attention to how language, however inadvertently, influences judgment. Even the name of the commission implied that "unreasonable accommodations" were being made and the majority needed to determine something more "reasonable."

Most of the so called accommodations that raised alarm, however, had involved innocuous requests, such as a Muslim group asking for a pork-free menu at Quebec sugar shacks,[130] similar to vegan clients requesting an adapted menu, or requests to accommodate a

---

129 "Bouchard–Taylor Commission Final Report Presentation," *CPAC*, May 22, 2008, https://www.cpac.ca/en/programs/public-record/episodes/14595692/.

130 In 2007, the sugar shack Érablière Au Pain de Sucre in Saint-Jean-sur-Richelieu removed pork from its pea soup for its Muslim clients, but kept the pork and beans and traditional *oreilles de Christ* (literally "Christ's ears," consisting of deep-fried fatback) on the menu for non-Muslims. The accommodations to the traditional fare was judged "unacceptable" by l'Association des restaurateurs des cabanes à sucre du Québec which stated there was no question of removing pork from traditional menus. Fast-forward to 2021 and the number of Quebec sugar shacks offering pork-free, vegan, and vegetarian options has mushroomed as the industry adapted to increased demand. Owners quickly saw a 30 to 40 percent increase in customers. "Des accommodements raisonables à la cabane à sucre!" *TVA Nouvelles*, March 19, 2007, https://www.tvanouvelles.ca/2007/03/19/des-accommodements-raisonnables-a-la-cabane-a-sucre.

peanut allergy. Requests that any smart business would quickly grant.

In the end, the report concluded that there was "no real crisis with the practice of accommodation in Quebec" and suggested that certain exceptions and requests for religious accommodations (most of them, ironically, made by Christian groups) had been highly mediatized, resulting only in the *perception* of a threat.

Recent attempts to limit immigration in Quebec have been messy, to say the least. In 2019, Quebec passed Bill 9, legislation to reform the immigration system, leading to the decision that 18,000 applications—representing close to 50,000 people—would be thrown out, with no consideration given to the efforts made, the years waiting or the costs incurred. Premier Legault indicated that he would be returning the application fees, as if that meagre amount could even begin to compensate for the fact that people's lives had been turned upside down.

Forcing 18,000 skilled workers to restart a lengthy and costly process, and setting out the framework for a new Quebec values test that economic immigration applicants would need to pass in order to become permanent residents, was not only cruel and damaging to Quebec's international reputation. In effect, it completely ignored the province's labour needs.[131] Higher education administrators and business communities reacted with alarm, warning the government that treating immigrants like disposable commodities would just motivate them to apply somewhere else.

---

131 Benjamin Shingler, "Quebec Will Make Immigrants Pass 'Values Test,'" *CBC News*, October 30, 2019, https://www.cbc.ca/news/canada/montreal/quebec-values-test-immigration-1.5340652.

A few months later, the Legault government would follow Bill 9 with a proposal to restrict access to a popular student immigration program, known as the Programme de l'expérience québécoise (PEQ) or Quebec Experience Program (QEP). Created in 2010, the program allowed foreign students and people working in the province for more than a year a fast-track toward permanency. Once again, public criticism was extensive. Montreal Board of Trade President, Michel Leblanc, said "limiting the numbers of international applicants would impoverish Quebec's future."

There was also extensive backlash from academia and business groups who saw the legislation as retrograde, and the CAQ was forced to backtrack. But it was too little too late for many highly educated, trilingual applicants who, with no desire to start from scratch, left the province. They lost out, and so did we.

The Quebec government's reticence to heed the warnings of business groups and labour statistics analysts could have long-standing consequences for the province's future economic prosperity. In another example, a Quebec Labour Market Forecast to 2025, commissioned by the Canadian Agricultural Human Resources Council (CAHRC), found that the province is expected to experience major labour shortages over the next decade. It reads,

> In 2014, labour shortages cost Quebec's agricultural sector an estimated $116 million, or 1.4% of sales. Based on a survey of the province's agricultural employers: 34% could not find enough workers, 34% were impacted by overtime costs, and

19% experienced production losses. Even with help from the foreign labour force, the province's agricultural sector was still unable to fill 3,300 jobs in 2014. The Council projects that as many as 19,900 jobs are at risk of going unfilled by 2029 as a result of a rapidly shrinking labour pool, significantly impacting the profitability and growth potential of the province's agriculture sector.[132]

In early 2022, a report by the Institut de la statistique du Québec revealed that one in five jobs in Quebec was now held by an immigrant, indicating their importance to the labour market. Despite this, a number of pundits routinely present immigration as the worst thing to happen to this province. Sociologist Mathieu Bock-Côté uses his considerable platform to rail against "massive" immigration and the minority groups who demand inclusion in political debates, claiming it undermines majority rule and prevents Quebec from attaining a collective identity. To him, minority identity and grievances are "imported from the US" and creations of a "radical left woke agenda."

That kind of attitude often comes from a place of deep insecurity; what novelist Toni Morrison defines so eloquently as the "fear of absorption, the horror of cultural embrace." Once measures have been put in place to strengthen and prioritize the language and ensure immigrants' integration into Quebec culture, Quebecers don't need to spend their entire lives in fear; on the contrary, the province needs immigrants.

---

132 "Quebec Agricultural Labour Market Forecast to 2025," *Canadian Agricultural Human Resources Council*, 2015.

In 1959, Quebec had the highest birthrate in the country, but after the Quiet Revolution it plummeted; by 1986, it hit a record low of 1.37 children per woman. In 2016, it hovered around 1.59. While I'm not interested in treating women and their uteri as objects of demographic policy, it's important to point out that a rate of at least 2.1 births is required for a population to replace itself. With this in mind, and also noting that Quebec has an aging population, this society must rely on immigration to maintain both its demographic weight and the affordability, quality, and availability of the services we have come to expect and pride ourselves in.

In the fall of 2021, when the proposed redistribution of parliamentary ridings was announced, Quebec was the only province to potentially lose a seat. If the seat is lost, Legault will lead a wave of discontentment; if it is preserved, Trudeau will be accused of doing too much for Quebec.[133] But ridings aren't allocated based on who's more "deserving," they're redrawn to reflect population changes. While the rest of Canada increased immigration by 6 percent, Quebec reduced it by a whopping 21 percent. Legault was unable (more likely, unwilling) to understand that his own party's decisions had compromised the province's demographic weight within Canada.

Considering current demographics (by 2031, a quarter of the province's population will be sixty-five years and older) and our low birth rate, Quebec's future depends upon increasing immigration and increased integration. We are cutting off our nose to spite our face.

---

133 John Ibbitson, "Trudeau's Decision over Quebec Seat Puts Him at Risk Either Way," *The Globe and Mail*, November 1, 2021.

Quebec needs immigration for "its heart to keep on beating," as poet and politician Gérald Godin so elegantly stated in his lyrical ode to immigration, *Tango de Montréal*. Not only do we need people to physically migrate, we need them to feel like they are part of the whole. Social cohesion doesn't result from government-appointed integration, guilt trips, parades or flag waving. Social cohesion happens when people feel they are recognized and appreciated for who they are. And who they are includes their parents, friends, and communities—their mothers who wear hijabs, their dads who may only speak Cantonese, their parishes, their mosques, and their festivals.

If you grow up feeling marginalized, your mother tongue vilified, your religion regarded with suspicion and erased from state institutions, your loyalty questioned every time you dare utter criticism, you won't feel like you belong. You won't feel like a Quebecer because you're not allowed to feel like one. If that happens, the onus isn't on those who feel marginalized. The onus is on the majority who made them feel that way.

16. Secularism or Intolerance?

What I remember most about attending Greek school as a child in Canada was how closely tied it was to the Greek Orthodox faith. We were taught Greek poems and songs, Greek Orthodox prayers, and pretty much anything that could turn us into Greeks who would be proud of our culture and work hard to maintain it and, in turn, teach it to the many kids that we were, of course, destined to have. I was an avid reader and adored Greek mythology, history, and literature, so those topics came easily to me. But religion left me indifferent.

I was an atheist by the age of seven, had a full-blown existential crisis at the age of eight—complete with a six-month bout of insomnia when I realized we all eventually die—and by the age of sixteen knew I wasn't interested in having kids. I simply didn't have the psychological and emotional makeup to believe that everything you were born and raised in was far superior to anything else you might encounter. As studious and polite a pupil as I was, I was also the teachers' worst nightmare.

I loved it all, mind you, but in the same way I loved the Catholic School I attended five days a week. I was upset when my friends got to prepare for Holy Communion so, not telling my parents or our Greek Orthodox priest, I participated in confession and took the wafer. I felt strongly that I belonged to it all and it all belonged to me.

While I eventually decided I preferred Greek Orthodox communion, with its spoonful of Mavrodaphne wine and sweet bread, I liked the idea of confessing my seven-year-old sins with the Catholics. I made up fake fights with my brother just to have something to say to the priest.

Looking back, it is ironic that an atheist doubled up on her church events simply because she enjoyed the rituals. I still do. Wherever I go in the world I visit the churches and mosques and temples and never cease to marvel at the beauty of faith and what some of us are compelled to create in some God's name.

I have heard the trance-inducing clang of a Buddhist bowl, the Torah recited at a synagogue, and choirs and sermons in Christian churches. I have listened to the Muslim muezzin's call to prayer as the old colonial port town of Penang, Malaysia, woke up. The sound of the *adhan*, or the call to worship, felt so similar to the Greek Orthodox Church's Byzantine chants of my youth, it brought me joy. I love Gregorian chants and enjoy Christmas mass. I annually get invited to Sukkot at my Jewish friend's house, have kneeled in reverence to Buddhist gods in Vietnam, and lit candles in memory of lost loved ones in tiny, humble chapels around the world. Even if I don't believe that God is great, *Allahu akbar* has only ever sounded to me like a simple greeting and benign welcome to worship.

One can reject the faith and all the often-dangerous and outdated trappings of organized religion but still respect the beauty and the human desire for meaning that it so often represents. I can understand the appeal of that kind of peace, even if I'm immune to it. Not everything is to be discarded or feared simply because it is not meant for you or because it's different.

In Quebec, much of the Roman Catholic faith and its practice was discarded in the Quiet Revolution of the 1960s. Quebec's acrimonious history with religion is the legacy of the Catholic Church's stranglehold over the French-speaking population, which was all-encompassing. The church forced women into having baby after baby; conspired with the British to gain influence and power; and kept the French-speaking population unschooled, uncultured, and in servitude.

Today, Quebec's religion is anti-religion. People seek to eradicate any display of excessive belief with dogma-like conviction, convinced that any religious adherence is fanaticism and dangerous. Where once this included the church, today Quebec's aversion to religion is limited to religions beyond the Catholic faith. Since Catholicism is now respected as part of the province's heritage (its *patrimoine*) only Muslim, Sikh, and Jewish Quebecers are required to sacrifice the visible symbols of their faith as per Bill 21. Notably, this policy only pertains to government bodies and public schools. Private schools can continue as they please, even though they receive government subsidies.

In 2017, a video of Muslim community members praying outdoors at Parc Safari—a popular Quebec zoo and amusement park—made the rounds, prompting outrage by onlookers who suspected, despite claims it was just an innocuous display of faith, that it was meant to be a deliberate and malicious provocation.

Most of the comments floating around went along the lines of, "Why do these people always flaunt their religion and throw it in our faces?", "Can't they keep this stuff private?" and "We need to ensure the separation of religion and public spaces."

On December 12, 2017, a *TVA Nouvelles* report alleged that female construction workers had been removed from a construction site near two Montreal mosques. According to the story, the demand was made by mosque administrators who didn't want women near their place of worship during Friday prayers. The alleged request targeted five women—four traffic control signallers and one engineer.

The public outrage was immediate and politicians deplored the incident as completely unacceptable. Within hours, a Facebook event page called for a protest in front of the mosque. Extreme far-right hate group *La Meute* stated they would join the protest to "show these people that here in Quebec men and women have the same rights and [they] won't tolerate such disrespect towards Quebec women."[134]

The only problem? None of it was true. The media outlet had never bothered to fact-check with the very people they were accusing, nor did they approach them for a single comment. Basic principles of journalism went out the window in the quest for a sensationalistic scoop and online clicks, thanks to Islamophobia putting the wind in that report's sails.

Two days after the *TVA* story, I wrote about my many misgivings in my then-weekly column in the *National*

---

134 Catherine Solyom, "Construction Commission Says Women Weren't Barred from Site," *The Gazette*, December 15, 2017.

Observer.[135] I specifically elaborated on why misinformation that feeds people's prejudices can be dangerous for those targeted. Even more baffling, the Quebec City mosque shooting, where six innocent men had been killed and nineteen others injured in their place of prayer, had taken place earlier that year and had been, in large part, fueled by Islamophobic rhetoric found online. Had we learned nothing?

A full year after the report, *TVA Nouvelles* admitted the story was unfounded and quietly recanted. Few paid attention to the apology. For the average reader who scanned the story and then forgot about it, it may well remain true in their minds.

Every year on Good Friday I take part in a religious procession called the Epitafio. This involves a large flower-decorated tomb of Christ mounted on tall poles solemnly carried around quiet streets while the faithful follow behind loudly chanting in ancient Greek, carrying incense and candles like a peaceful, well-dressed cult. The very next night, my community sets off firecrackers outside our churches in residential neighbourhoods to celebrate Greek Easter. There's nothing either private or quiet about loud religious incantations, a thousand candles being lit up all at once, or midnight firecrackers. Yet, I have never heard anyone say a peep about these religious customs.

The only difference between a group of Muslims praying in an outdoor park and a group of Greek Orthodox doing the same, is the difference between

---

135 Toula Drimonis, "Questionable *TVA* Story a Reminder of Media's Responsibility to Report Carefully," *National Observer*, December 14, 2017.

what is considered benignly foreign versus what's seen as menacing. This equation changes from generation to generation. In most cases, the only way something transitions from scary to ordinary is time and familiarity.

To claim that public displays of religion don't have a place here is a lie. Religion is everywhere, from the 131-metre-high illuminated cross staring down at us from Mount Royal to the bells from the Roman Catholic church around the corner; to the crucifixes in hospitals and courthouses, to saints' names for every second street and school.

The very same year the Parc Safari incident happened, Montreal was celebrating its 375th anniversary. The event was ostentatiously marked with the symbolic sounding of St. Joseph's Oratory's first bell, followed by the simultaneous chiming of church bells across Montreal for *ten entire minutes*. A public mass was held at the Oratory, where priests, deacons, members of religious communities, and special guests were all in attendance. Imagine for just one minute that something similarly invasive, loud, and public was held in the Muslim community and its places of worship.

On April 12th, 2019, a Facebook post claimed cafés in Montreal's Petit Maghreb neighbourhood (an area with large Tunisian, Algerian, and Moroccan populations) were refusing to serve women. Within hours, it was shared more than 2,600 times, followed by online threats. One in particular, Café Sable d'or, was targeted by a series of bad *Yelp* reviews and hateful comments on its website, with people denouncing the establishment as proof of "Islamic integration," and reminding the owner that "this is Quebec, not some Islamist barbaric country where women have to submit to men."[136]

Baffled café owners denied the accusations and wondered how that rumour started. Thankfully, some quick sleuthing by *Radio-Canada* confirmed the story was a lie. Adding insult to injury, the person who posted the initial status lived hours away from Montreal and had never even visited the area, nor had he any tangible proof that access had been denied women. He had "just heard it from someone else."

A similar situation had occurred in France the year before, when television channel *France 2* reported that women were not welcome in bars in the Maghrebi community of Sevran, a suburb of Paris. Investigations proved those allegations false.

I'm still amazed that any of these stories were published with little corroborating information or even confirmation. The reason these "reports" aren't questioned is that they feed into assumptions about Islam. *Of course,* the mosque had forbidden women to be on the construction site! *Of course,* they are religious fanatics who must flaunt their faith! *Of course,* Muslim café owners are forbidding women to enter their premises!

Notwithstanding Premier François Legault's denials, Islamophobia is a problem in the province and across Canada. A 2017 Angus Reid poll revealed 46 percent of Canadians held unfavourable views of Islam as opposed to other faiths.[137] A *Radio-Canada* poll conducted the

136 Bouchra Ouatik, "Non, les cafés du Petit Maghreb ne sont pas interdits aux femmes," *Radio-Canada*, April 12, 2019.
137 Adam Frisk, "Nearly Half of Canadians View Islam Unfavourably, Survey Finds," *Global News*, April 4, 2017.

same year found 23 percent of Canadians favoured a ban on Muslim immigration. That number climbs to 32 percent in Quebec.[138] Anti-Muslim sentiment appeared to be the main motivation behind Bill 21 support, with 88 percent of those holding negative views of Islam in favour of a ban on religious symbols for schoolteachers. "Conversely, those who held positive views of those religions were overwhelmingly against the ban."[139]

Far too many people continue to confuse the Muslim faith with Islamic extremism, which is akin to confusing your run-of-the-mill church-going auntie with Christian fundamentalists who insist COVID-19 is "God's way to hold us guilty for abortion and same-sex marriage."[140]

But, while most people have ample examples of "benign" Christianity, too often they are swayed by caricatures and fear-inducing examples of Islam. It's precisely why these numbers go way down when you poll younger people. They have been raised in a multicultural environment and have been exposed to a variety of "others" in ways that the older generations were not. They don't fear what they already know. To a young Quebecer, a classmate with a hijab isn't a symbol of religious extremism. She's just Houda from Hochelaga who likes Charlotte Cardin and excels in math.

In the early days of the COVID-19 pandemic, neighbourhood churches rang their bells at all hours of the

---

138 Kamila Hinkson, Kalina Laframboise, "Canadians Divided When it Comes to Immigration, Poll Suggests," *CBC News*, March 13, 2017.
139 Jason Magder, "A New Poll Shows Support for Bill 21 is Built on Anti-Islam Sentiment," *The Gazette*, May 18, 2019.
140 Brian Niemietz, "Evangelist Pat Robertson Says Coronavirus is God's Way to 'Hold us Guilty' for Abortion, Same Sex Marriage," *New York Daily News*, April 21, 2020.

day, every day, to soothe the residents. When religious services in places of worship were banned to respect social distancing measures, some cities allowed outdoor celebrations or facilitated exterior displays of faith. Church services across the country were Zoomed, or held in parking lots and on front steps. But when multiple Canadian cities allowed (for the first time ever, in most cases) the *adhan*, the Muslim call for prayer, to be announced over mosque loudspeakers so the community in lockdown could hear it during Ramadan, some people reacted with the level of horror reserved for an ISIS invasion.

In the western part of Montreal's Mile End neighbourhood, where the Hasidic Jewish population hovers at around 30 percent, the ultra-Orthodox sects had to find creative ways to continue to pray together. To get around the restrictions, they began singing and praying from their balconies and front stoops, creating a form of outdoor synagogue. While most people found it charming to witness what is usually done in private, some expressed their frustration, anger, and distaste. They didn't want to be "exposed" to these alien traditions.[141]

Throughout the early months of the pandemic, suspicious citizens were calling the police to investigate infractions in synagogues and mosques. Among them, Quebec historian, Dawson College professor, and onetime PQ candidate Frédéric Bastien, who posted on social media during the first lockdown that, according to "his sources," Montreal police had to put an end to an illegal religious ceremony at the Islamic Centre of Quebec (ICQ) in Ville Saint-Laurent that violated

---

141 Rima Elkouri, "Les chants du balcon," *La Presse*, May 6, 2020.

pandemic rules. Eleven fines were issued against the mosque, he said.

None of it was true. Even the image Bastien used on his Facebook page had nothing to do with the incident, but was from January 2017 when police were at the mosque to offer protection following the Quebec City mosque massacre committed by Alexandre Bissonnette.

Three days after Bastien's post, Lamine Foura, an Algerian Quebecer who works as an engineer at Bombardier and is the founder of *Médias Maghreb*, a local news outlet for the Maghrebi community, called the Montreal police (SPVM) to verify the events. He was informed that "no violation was found to have taken place and no fine was given." He let Bastien know on social media, but received no acknowledgement whatsoever.

The following day, May 15th, *Journal Métro* published an article also confirming that no fines had been issued, citing SPVM spokesperson André Durocher who called it a "non-event."[142] Bastien, who, according to political scientist Felix Mathieu, was supported by the most fervent secularist wing of the PQ party during his leadership run, eventually issued a mea culpa, but by then the original post had predictably elicited its share of hateful Islamophobic comments.

In April 2021, Bloc MP Xavier Barsalou-Duval shared a Facebook post expressing his shock that Canada Post had issued a stamp celebrating Ramadan. "While Quebec is promoting secularism, Canada is engaging in religious indoctrination," he wrote. "There is no way out... this

---

142 Laurent Lavoie, "Confusion autour d'une intervention policière à Saint-Laurent," *Métro,* May 15, 2020.

country is a madhouse." The stamp was one of an annual series celebrating all religious holidays. Meanwhile, the Bloc issues Christmas and Easter wishes to their constituents every year, and an image in the MP's Facebook timeline shows him happily signing Christmas cards. Barsalou-Duval was not bothered by the stamps with Christmas nativity scenes.

How did Quebec go from "religion shouldn't influence government decisions" to having an elected official hyperventilating at the sight of a stamp and equating it to religious indoctrination? This isn't secularism, this is intolerance. In such a setting, any small attempts to establish your faith and build your place of worship is seen as encroachment. Just think of how long it took for the Quebec town of Saint-Apollinaire to finally vote to allow for a Muslim cemetery to be built in 2017—and just think of how little we've heard of it since it was approved.[143]

We accuse people of being loud and of taking over precisely because we don't hear the overbearingly loud sound of our own privilege. It doesn't register because it is familiar. You don't notice the sound of traffic or the hum of the refrigerator because it's just there and always has been. It's the background noise to our daily lives.

Isn't it fascinating that some forms of "loud" identity don't bother us, while others do. Think of the proud Italian Quebecer who decorates his car with an Italian flag, several icons of the Virgin Mary, and a huge sticker that says "*Italia. Campioni del Mondo.*" Even louder and

---

143 "Canada Town Votes Against Having a Muslim Cemetery," *BBC News*, July 18, 2017.

more obvious during the World Cup when his team scores. It's over the top, but it's harmless.

Now, think of a woman walking down the street minding her own business while wearing a hijab. To some people her mere presence is an outright provocation. Why does she flaunt her faith? Why is she asking for more accommodations, more concessions, more visibility?

As an ardent feminist, I don't care for any symbol of women's subjugation and inequality. But people who think that hijabs and niqabs (and the most extreme of them all, burkas) are the only examples of religious subjugation of women are blind. There isn't a single major religion that doesn't at some point treat women as inferior, impure, or threatening. Policing of women's bodies and behaviours continues to be a time-honoured tradition around the world, no matter the culture or faith. Women will always wear too much or too little. They will always be asked to abide by some ill-defined and ever-changing societal rule about what they should wear, how they should behave, and what their rights and privileges are. If you find this complicated to follow, I have a guideline that applies in all situations with regards to what women wear or how they behave: *it's none of our business.*

French Quebecers have such negative connotations of organized religion, thanks to their experience of the Roman Catholic church, that they have a hard time understanding that someone can have a willing, healthy, and beneficial relationship with faith. French Quebecers' trauma (for lack of a better word) manifests itself as extreme distrust of religion and a bizarre insistence that not being exposed to public displays of other religions in the public sphere is somehow a right. The irony, of course, is that this demand is made while symbols of Christianity are pervasive, prioritized, and protected.

17. Les autres

Je les entends, une chronique après l'autre. Mais après combien de fois, aurai-je enfin le droit de ne plus t'expliquer que je viens d'ici, moi? Que je suis aussi chez moi?

I hear them, one column after another. But after how many times will I finally have the right to no longer have to explain to you that this is where I come from? That I, too, am home?[144]

—Cathy Wong, "Monstrueuse," Monstrueuse/SLAM

The question of *othering* is complicated in Quebec. The province's unique position as a linguistic minority within the larger English-speaking majority places it in the position of having to define itself in relation to others, forever juxtaposed against the political and linguistic framework of the rest of Canada (ROC) and its overriding power.

This often means that discussions of race, racism (systemic or otherwise), xenophobia, nationalism, secularism and religious intolerance don't take place

---

144 Cathy Wong, "Monstrueuse/SLAM," in *Libérer la colère*, eds. Geneviève Morand and Natalie-Ann Roy (Montreal: Éditions du remue-ménage, 2018). Cathy Wong is a former Montreal city councillor and speaker of the Montreal City Council.

in Quebec without some politicians and pundits derailing the conversation for fear that it will provide ammunition to those who disparage the province. Many are unable to see the difference between merited political criticism and so-called "Quebec bashing."

In addition, as in the rest of Canada, history has been whitewashed in Quebec, downplaying colonialism, slavery and harm done to Indigenous communities. French Quebec's historical narrative is a reductive one, consisting almost exclusively of the French struggle against English colonialism and oppression. Most people complete their formal education having never learned that more than four thousand enslaved people (Black and Indigenous) were documented in Quebec; as a result, many insist that slavery and racism are US imports and have nothing to do with us. Quebecers refuse to see their own role in the historic and systemic discrimination against Indigenous communities within the province's borders. Pointing to the federal Indian Act, we like to absolve ourselves of any wrongdoing. This is a comforting lie, considering that we have been complicit in residential schools, medical colonialism, discrimination, and racism.

When the Quebec Liberal Party announced that a public consultation on systemic racism would finally get underway in 2017, after repeated requests by representatives of Quebec's Black, Muslim, and Indigenous communities, reactions ranged from denial to anger to accusations. The Parti Québécois complained that the consultation would put "Quebecers on trial."

Through the prism of Quebec history and nationalism, many Quebecers have somehow managed to divorce French settlement from colonial violence, conquest, and dispossession. Quebec nationalists do not see themselves as being in a position of power within the Canadian federation and therefore are never guilty of holding the upper hand in any possible system of discrimination. How can one be both the oppressed and the oppressor? It's simple. Being the former doesn't cancel out the latter. It is possible to be many things simultaneously.

Many Quebec nationalists, feeling attacked, tend to close ranks, making them particularly vulnerable to populism. Quebec nationalists enjoy quoting Pierre Vallières's 1968 book *N***** blancs d'Amérique* (*White N***** of America*), because it equates the French Quebec struggle for equal rights and social agency with the American civil rights movement of the 60s. There was, indeed, a strong affinity between Quebec nationalism and the struggle by African Americans for equal rights in the 60s. Many Quebec student unions rallied in support of Selma protesters in 1965, and the Rassemblement pour l'indépendance nationale (RIN) frequently used sit-ins as a protest gesture at restaurants and places of business, a tactic borrowed from the US civil-rights movement.

However, by continuing to conflate class exploitation with slavery in this misleading analogy, it offers the depiction of a legitimate class struggle as a historical alibi for French colonialism and the oppression of Aboriginal peoples. It also ignores the cries from many

Black activists in Quebec calling out racism and discrimination right here at home.[145]

Even Vallières later regretted the comparison and worried that French Quebec ethno-nationalism could degenerate into a xenophobic form of populism. He grew disenchanted with the PQ and didn't vote in the 1980 referendum, and the 1990 standoff during the Oka Crisis "forced him to take a stance *for* the Mohawks and *against* the Quebec state and [he] even [went] as far as advocating for Indigenous rights to self-determination and sovereignty."[146] By the end of his life, Vallières took on the causes of gay rights, mental health, and native self-government. While he still hoped for Quebec independence, he believed that a Quebec hostile to immigrants did not deserve to survive.[147]

English-speaking and allophone minorities are often perceived as having ulterior motives and acting in bad faith when they express valid criticism of Quebec. However, one rarely sees accusations of "Quebec bashing" lobbed against French-speaking Quebecers who

---

145 "While Québécois nationalists and other Francophone observers followed the American civil rights movement, Black Power and other Black-centered anticolonial political tendencies very closely, and used those bodies of theory as a way to think about their own struggle, there were comparatively few debates about Black rights in Canada, or discussions involving West Indians, African-Americans, Black African students or white African settlers that unfolded in Montreal's Francophone press." Paul C. Hébert, "A Microcosm of the General Struggle," in *Black Thought and Activism in Montreal, 1960-1969* (Doctoral thesis, University of Michigan, 2015), 13.

146 Bruno Cornellier, "The Struggle of Others: Pierre Vallières, Québécois Settler Nationalism, and the N-Word Today," *Discourse: Journal for Theoretical Studies in Media and Culture* Vol. 39, No. 1 (Winter 2017), 31-66.

147 Michel Lapierre, "'Dissident': Pierre Vallières, chercheur d'absolu," *Le Devoir*, November 10, 2018.

publicly voice concerns or share difficult truths. The following example does a good job of highlighting the *deux poids, deux mesures* constantly at play.

In the winter of 2017, former journalist and then-director of the McGill Institute for the Study of Canada, Andrew Potter, wrote a scathing column for *Maclean's* exposing "the essential malaise eating away at the foundations of Quebec society."[148] Potter described Quebec as an "almost pathologically alienated and low-trust society, deficient in many of the most basic forms of social capital that other Canadians take for granted."

I remember being dumbfounded after I reached the end of that piece. It was deeply insulting, ill-conceived, and unfair to Quebecers. I still don't know what Potter (himself married to a Quebecer and living in Montreal for years) was thinking when he wrote it. Sure, Quebec can sometimes be a mess, but no more so than any other province in this country.

Faced with intense scrutiny from the public, pundits, and even politicians, including calls for his resignation, Potter eventually left his position, though he stayed on at McGill as a professor. He publicly retracted his article and apologized for it, but it was too late. The damage was done.

Ironically, the very next day, a popular Quebec French-language columnist wrote a similar article about what a hot mess this province was. "Their old people die in shit, people are asphyxiated in their cars, they can't even manage in a snowstorm, and civil servants are paid to do nothing… Quebec is the paradise of comics and

---

148 Andrew Potter, "How a Snowstorm Exposed Quebec's Real Problem: Social Malaise," *Maclean's*, March 20, 2017.

caricaturists. The place is a bloody mess, but boy, do they ever laugh."[149]

Barely a shrug from French-language pundits or Quebec politicians about that column, "Nous vivons dans un film de Denys Arcand," by Richard Martineau. Yet the language was equally harsh and insulting, and the message more or less the same. *Gazette* political columnist Don Macpherson wrote a very astute piece asking why Martineau wasn't being accused of "Quebec bashing" for his column, yet Potter had the entire province up in arms. "The vehemence of the reaction to it, and the indifference to Martineau's similar column, show that Potter's real crime is not what he wrote; it's who wrote it, the language in which he wrote it, and for whom he wrote it."[150]

Even though the term "Québécois" is supposed to delineate a civic, rather than an ethnic or linguistic identity, and even though leaders of Quebec's independence movement have often repeated that a Quebecer is whoever wants to be a Quebecer, it doesn't often play out that way.

Filmmaker Pierre Falardeau, appearing on the television show *Tout le monde en parle* in 2008, was asked to explain an opinion piece he wrote complaining that young immigrants live in their "multicultural bubbles," having no contact with Quebecers in their "cosmopolitan ghettos." In doing so, he shared that he had recently given a talk at Louis-Joseph-Papineau high school,

149 Richard Martineau, "Nous vivons dans un film de Denys Arcand," *Le Journal de Montréal*, March 21, 2017.

150 Don Macpherson, "Andrew Potter and la famille Québécoise," *The Gazette*, March 23, 2017.

located in Saint-Michel, one of Montreal's poorest districts, and how "60 percent of the students are Haitian, 30 percent are Latino, and the only Québécois was the teacher."

To their credit, both host Guy Lepage and then-sidekick Dany Turcotte immediately responded that all these kids *were* Québécois, having been born here and living here now. Falardeau replied, "I've lived in Quebec's Northern Territories (Le Grand Nord) and that doesn't make me an Eskimo."[151] Pressured by Lepage and Turcotte, he explained, "it's not enough to live here and pay taxes here, you need to integrate." By integration, Falardeau meant support for Quebec's independence movement. In other words, unless you are a very specific kind of Quebecer, you don't pass the authenticity test. Furthermore, if you're a French Quebecer and don't vote for sovereignty, you're an "imbecile" and a "cretin."[152] Good to know that he was an equal-opportunity insulter.

This continues to be the theme in Quebec nationalist politics today, where "Quebec values" and "Quebec culture" are defined by a select few. If you're a federalist, an advocate for multiculturalism, a believer in the benefits of bilingualism, or someone who has no issues with hijabs on teachers and therefore opposed to Bill 21, you aren't a "true" Quebecer. I once saw a francophone expressing pity for Quebec federalists on Twitter because, for him, "they were abuse victims who had developed a strange form of Stockholm syndrome."

151 The word Eskimo is an offensive term that has been used historically to describe the Inuit, but has been left here as it's a direct quote.

152 Martin Patriquin, "Separatism Weakening in Quebec," *Maclean's*, September 6, 2007.

More recently, another artist, Quebec stand-up comedian and actor Adib Alkhalidey was on the same show, discussing how let down he felt as a second-generation Arab immigrant, watching Quebec refuse to have important debates on diversity and systemic racism, and constantly accusing those who did bring these issues up of "Quebec bashing."

"I'm in my thirties and I grew up in Ville Saint-Laurent," he told Lepage, "and ten-year-olds today are living the same things I did when I was ten. They don't watch TV because they don't see themselves." He went on to say that "we're depriving an entire generation… of the right to belong to Quebec, the right to identify with Quebec culture. They are stateless, even though they're born here, because they don't see themselves anywhere."

People need to be allowed plurality, diversity, and representation, and they need to be seen and recognized for what and who they are—without limitations or ultimatums. Being made to feel like you don't belong unless you adhere to specific conditions is deeply counterproductive not only for social cohesion but also for an individual's mental health and happiness. It takes a terrible toll to be constantly forced to defend your identity and your place in a society.

When Premier Legault claimed Liberal Party leader Dominique Anglade was "incapable of defending Quebec values" after she stated that her party would not renew Bill 21's notwithstanding clause and would let the courts decide, he was in dangerous populist territory.[153]

---

153 Marc-André Gagnon, "Anglade est incapable de défendre les valeurs des Québécois, dit Legault," *Le Journal de Québec*, April 22, 2021.

Whose values does he think he is defending? Are Legault (and the CAQ, a party voted in with only 37 percent of the vote) the arbiters of everything Québécois? Is Anglade, a Black woman with Haitian-born parents, not a Quebecer? Are the people fighting to strike down Bill 21 not Quebecers? Are members of Montreal City Council, who in rare unanimity adopted a resolution condemning Bill 21 not Quebecers? The ultimate irony is that Bill 21 required the use of the notwithstanding clause *precisely* because it goes against Quebec values, more specifically the Quebec Charter of Rights and Freedoms, upon which the Canadian Charter is modelled.

In the fall of 2021, the CAQ announced that it would be replacing the high school Ethics and Religious Cultures course with one that would focus only on Quebec culture and citizenship. There's nothing wrong with students learning about Quebec culture and how to be better citizens. The problem for many teachers and parents was the fact that it would be replacing a course whose aim is to expose students to *other* cultures and religions, in essence equipping them for a multicultural and pluralistic world. Public Security Minister Geneviève Guilbault went so far as to affirm that the new course would be taught with a dose of chauvinism, raising red flags for many.[154]

Aggressive nationalism creates distrust and intolerance of difference. Moreover, refusing to teach about an increasingly pluralistic world is to fail the students from the start. Whatever we ourselves believe, we unquestionably live in a diverse world with people who have

---

154 Alexandre Sirois, "Le chauvinisme, la pensée critique et nos enfants," *La Presse*, October 25, 2021.

different beliefs. Learning about other religions and cultures isn't indoctrination, it's increasing cultural tolerance and understanding of others. Social cohesion and harmony *requires* that of us.

The CAQ's constant need to create an official party line that defines the *one* way to be a Quebecer means outsiders will be scrutinized and assessed accordingly. When tensions rise, those buttons will be pushed even more.

Homogeneity or even consensus cannot be requirements for belonging in a society. We need to leave room for difference and for dissent. That goes for immigrants wanting to be recognized as true members of this society, for Quebec's ever-shrinking English-speaking minority still seen as the enemy by some (and who *Gazette* columnist Brendan Kelly described as a "phantom opponent"), and it even goes for French speakers in the rest of Canada who are often subjected to *actual* Quebec bashing by people who know little about their history, their reality, and their fears.

18. Muslim Women, Bill 21, and Othering

> We love our school, our city, our neighbourhood,
> we love our province, but sometimes I don't feel
> the love back.
>
> —Hiba Jabouirik, Muslim Quebecer

No better current example of *othering* exists in Quebec than Bill 21, the province's secularism legislation that bans the wearing of religious symbols—the Muslim hijab, the Jewish kippah, the Sikh dastar—by people in positions of authority in the public service, such as teachers and police.

By *pre-emptively* discriminating based on the hypothetical possibility of religious extremism, Bill 21 is meant to appease Quebec's largely anti-religious base. This, despite the fact that judicial reviews exist if judges exhibit a lack of impartiality and objectivity; teachers are required to follow the Basic School Regulation and are prohibited from proselytizing; and there are zero documented cases in the province of a person in authority, wearing said symbols, attempting to use that authority to impose their religion. [155]

---

155 Sidhartha Banerjee, "Quebec High Court Rules Judge Wrong to Order Woman to Remove Hijab," *The Canadian Press*, October 3, 2018.

I have written numerous columns over the years defending Quebec's often-progressive vision and politics. But after Bill 21 was adopted, I felt betrayed by my own government. As an atheist, a member of an ethnic minority, and the daughter of immigrants, I was deeply ashamed of the place I call home.

Simon Jolin-Barrette, Quebec's then-Minister of Immigration, Francisation, and Integration—the lawyer who invoked the notwithstanding clause, allowing his government to circumvent sections of the Charter of Rights and Freedoms to force through Bill 21—was the perfect foot soldier. He never seemed to care about the lives affected or the fact that his legislation would embolden racists to engage in harassment and discrimination against people wearing visible religious symbols.

When Quebec feminist groups warned him during the bill's public hearings that minority women would be affected far more than men, Jolin-Barrette refused a request made by the Liberals, Québec Solidaire, and the City of Montreal to study whether the law he was proposing would have a differential impact on women.[156] During the weekend of June 16th, 2019, when both Bill 9 on immigration reforms and Bill 21 were fast-tracked by the CAQ via closure, Jolin-Barrette decided to go for a jog, a move denounced by all three opposition parties at the time as an indication of the government's arrogance.

"While we are here talking about the future of thousands of women, men and children, where is the minister

---

156 Jonathan Montpetit, "Religious Symbols Ban Pits Quebec Feminists Against Each Other," *CBC News*, May 16, 2019, https://www.cbc.ca/news/canada/montreal/bill-21-quebec-feminists-on-opposite-sides-of-religious-symbols-ban-1.5139422.

responsible for the bill?" [Liberal MNA, Marc] Tanguay said in remarks about Bill 9. "He is out jogging on the Plains of Abraham."[157]

During the public debates, Premier Legault even admitted that the deeply polarizing legislation was a concession to the majority of people who wanted secularism, and his government could have gone even further: "We are setting the limits, because there are some slightly racist people who would like there to be no religious symbols at all, not even in public spaces."[158]

For a province that places large crosses on mountains, it was the very definition of exclusionary populism. As a small concession (if one can call it that), Bill 21 allowed workers currently wearing religious symbols to be exempt from the law, but they lose their privileges if they change jobs or get promoted, essentially blocking them from any career mobility. The notwithstanding clause overrides the charter for a period of five years, but, not surprisingly, the legislation has already been challenged in court and partially struck down (the Quebec government is appealing).

Many of Bill 21's supporters insist the legislation is necessary to ensure gender equality in the province. To them, the hijab is a symbol of women's submission and religious dogma. They point to Muslim countries where women have been fighting for the right to remove it. But since when is legislation here enacted to fight laws elsewhere? Many Quebec feminists consider Bill 21 to be

---

157 Philip Authier, "Tensions Boil Over in National Assembly as Minister Goes Jogging During Debate," *The Gazette*, June 16, 2019.

158 Sophie-Hélène Lebeuf, «Laïcité : « pour éviter les extrêmes, il faut en donner un peu à la majorité, »" *La Presse*, June 18, 2019, https://ici. radio-canada.ca/nouvelle/1190230/francois-legault-entrevue-patrice-roy-laicite-bilan.

profoundly sexist and a form of colonization because it ultimately eliminates women's choice.

"As a feminist, I'm all for the state playing a role in furthering gender equality," Alexa Conradi, the former president of Quebec's most prominent women's rights organization, the Fédération des femmes du Québec (FFQ), explained in 2019. "You can accomplish that goal, however, by ensuring that women have access to work, access to decently paid work, access to daycare facilities and quality childcare services, and by fighting violence against women."[159]

Bill 21 legislators are operating under the false assumption that these women need saving. "While it's true that in some countries, women are forced to wear head coverings, that's not the case here," she added. "Legislating women to fit into a certain ideal of equality is paternalistic. There can certainly be a critique in our society of religious power and/or dogma, but it's never a good idea for the state to take over the role of how women should act and look."

In continued *othering*, the parliamentary committee to debate the legislation at the National Assembly barely included representation from those most affected.

"If I claim that I care about real equality between men and women, people will not want to hear me, because I am a Muslim woman, two realities that are incompatible according to some," writes Montreal lawyer Shahad

---

159 Toula Drimonis, "Sounding the Alarm on Quebec's Secularism Law," *National Observer*, June 7, 2019.

Salman in her essay "Qui Suis-Je" (Who am I), part of an anthology about anger written by Quebec women.[160]

The bill resulted in many of the consequences its detractors feared: increased marginalization, increased barriers to employment, economic precarity and social isolation for a group of women who already experience discrimination. Even before the bill became law, Muslim women in Quebec reported being followed and spat upon on the street, subjected to online harassment, and having strangers attempt to yank hijabs off their heads.[161] Many hijabi teachers left the province or changed careers, unwilling to be told how to live their lives. And this, amidst serious teacher shortages in the province.

In 2020, I interviewed Montreal teacher Mariam Aziz, who compared the CAQ's unconstitutional law to an abusive relationship where she felt undervalued and condescended to. Bill 21 forced her to walk away from teaching and a dream of pursuing a masters in education. She explains,

> How many nights had I stayed up while studying at McGill to make sure I made the Golden Key International Honour Society, to make sure I aced every exam, to make sure I had time to work as a specialized educator while completing my degree? How much effort had I put in to impress during my *stages* (internships), to make sure I was

---

160 Shahad Salman, "Qui Suis-Je," in *Libérer la colère*, eds. Geneviève Morand and Natalie-Ann Roy (Montreal : Éditions du remue-ménage, 2018).

161 Jonathon Montpetit, "Muslim Women Report Spike in Harassment, Discrimination since Bill 21 Tabled," *CBC*, May 14, 2019.

outstanding, to stay back after school and help with anything and everything I could to make sure I got a position? For what? When someone less qualified could in the future be promoted over me for the single reason that I wear a headscarf?[162]

She wasn't the only one who felt let down. A *Globe and Mail* feature titled "I Feel Like a Stranger Here Now" detailed the disillusionment and pain of six Quebec-born women who now felt like second-class citizens. Amrit Kaur, who is of Sikh faith and wears a turban, graduated with a teaching degree the day Bill 21 was passed into law. She relocated to BC after her dreams were dashed. Ironically, for those who defend Bill 21 as legislation that encourages gender equality, "Sikh women adopting the turban is a form of reclaiming equality as they're traditionally worn by men, in upholding one of Sikhism's articles of faith."[163]

Quebec politicians are often guilty of adding oil to the forever-simmering fire of Islamophobia. During his PQ leadership campaign in 2016, Jean-François Lisée justified the need for a ban on Muslim religious garbs by claiming that his primary responsibility as a premier would be to ensure the safety of all Quebecers and that a Muslim woman could easily hide an AK-47 machine gun under her burka.[164]

---

162 Toula Drimonis, "This Muslim Woman is Walking Away from a Teaching Career due to Bil 21," *Cult MTL*, June 23, 2020.

163 Amy Chung, "How Bill 21 Has Affected These Quebec Women in the Workplace," *Huffington Post*, August 3, 2021.

164 Robert Dutrisac, "Lisée propose une 'discussion' sur l'interdiction de la burqa," *Le Devoir*, September 17, 2016.

After Alexandre Bissonnette gunned down six men in prayer at the Quebec City mosque on January 29th, 2017, police looking through his browsing history quickly realized that his actions were influenced by a steady diet of far-right, anti-immigrant voices. Bissonnette was obsessed with Donald Trump and had searched for the US president online more than eight hundred times between January 1st and January 29th, the day of the shooting.

The pundits he consulted most were far-right network *Breitbart*'s Ben Shapiro, Alex Jones of *Infowars*, white nationalist Richard Spencer, and other known Islamophobes. When, two days after Trump imposed his anti-Muslim travel ban, Canadian Prime Minister Justin Trudeau tweeted he was ready to welcome Syrian immigrants fleeing persecution, Bissonnette was primed and ready to protect what he perceived was in danger.

"I was watching TV and learned that the Canadian government was going to take more refugees, you know, who couldn't go to the United States, and they were coming," he told *Sûreté du Québec* Sergeant Steve Girard in an interrogation clip that played at his sentencing hearing. "I saw that and lost my mind. I don't want them to kill my parents, my family."[165]

Even though there's no doubt that Bissonnette was a troubled young man, he was still the product of the media he consumed. Anti-immigrant punditry and right-wing online sites have become breeding and recruiting grounds for angry, scared young white men, radicalizing them and pushing them toward violence.

---

165 Toula Drimonis, "Bissonnette was a Far-Right Internet Junkie Whose Addiction Turned him into a Killer," *National Observer,* April 17, 2018.

Fear-mongering pundits and politicians nurture these seeds of hate.

In June of 2019, Liberal MNA for Bourassa-Sauvé, Paule Robitaille, was forced to delete a tweet that featured a smiling image of her with four female teachers-to-be who were wearing hijabs. In the tweet Robitaille wrote, "They are competent, intelligent, and adorable. Because of the secularism law, these women won't be able to teach in our schools. A loss for everyone." The internet, as they say, exploded.

"After seven hundred and fifty messages (most of them hateful) I was forced to delete my tweet at the request of one of the young women in the picture with me," she explained online. "This is the climate we have found ourselves in. This is not the Quebec that I know. We must welcome and integrate, not exclude."[166]

Those messages didn't materialize out of thin air. They were largely inspired by *Journal de Montréal* columnist Richard Martineau, who felt compelled to point out Robitaille's "bad faith" and therefore placed her on his followers' crosshairs. The people who claimed they enacted Bill 21 to save these women instead did the exact opposite.

Majority privilege often prevents people from realizing the impact of their actions because those actions never affect them. I trust the good (albeit, misguided) intentions of some defenders of Bill 21, but if the result is more marginalization for these women, their intentions don't matter. Instead of seeing Muslim women

166 Martin Patriquin, "Quebecers' double standard on women and their bodies," *The Gazette*, June 12, 2019.

who choose to wear the hijab as complex individuals possessing their own autonomy, they are treated by the Quebec government as either docile victims or demonized vectors of extremism. Never are they simply people making decisions that are different from our own. Like Kellie Leitch's Barbaric Cultural Practices tip line and Hérouxville's code of conduct, Bill 21 is a "solution" to a non-existent problem.

As Montreal North high-school teacher Vincent Ouellette demonstrated in 2020, just as the presence of religious symbols is not proof of religious zealotry, the absence of religious symbols cannot be mistaken for impartiality. In November of 2020, Ouellette was secretly filmed by a student gleefully and repeatedly hurling the N-word during an online class. After a video of the incident went viral, many of his current and former students came forward with numerous accusations of racism, Islamophobia, bigotry, and anti-immigrant sentiments over his twenty-year career.[167] Among the acts he committed was to insist that his Muslim students apologize for terrorism. Imagine singling out a fifteen-year-old child and demanding they personally account for violent acts thousands of miles away simply because they share the same religion!

Despite repeated complaints to authorities, Ouellette passed under the radar for years. Using his platform to spew hate did not raise red flags simply because he is the type of authority figure we have decided is "neutral" and "socially acceptable."

---

167 "Montreal North Teacher Fired after Repeatedly Saying the N-word in Class," *The Gazette*, November 22, 2020.

In his book *Deep Diversity*, Shakil Choudhury says, "the power to define normal is one of the systemic powers generally invisible to dominant groups."[168] Quebec's majority has decided that their "normal" is people who don't wear visible religious symbols, and that their "abnormal" is people who do.

168 Shakil Choudhury, *Deep Diversity: Overcoming Them vs. Us* (Toronto: Between the Lines, 2015), 40.

19. A Case for Multiculturalism

Multiculturalism has been an official federal government policy since 1971. Immigrants can retain and practice their customs, language, and religion without being penalized or persecuted. That means that when a Sikh Canadian wants to serve in the RCMP while wearing his turban, he won't be refused. If a Muslim Canadian woman wearing a hijab wants to become a judge or a police officer, she can.

Despite criticism that multiculturalism encourages ethnic differences or prevents integration by undermining social cohesion, it's rarely the case. Even though the demand for assimilation is not made, the transition—with few exceptions—eventually and almost inevitably happens. Any child of immigrants knows this, and every parent of second-generation offspring will grudgingly admit to it.

"I became a real Canadian gently, by osmosis. There was no pressure to conform to the new or repudiate the old," writes Cherif Rifaat in *Immigrants Adapt, Countries Adopt. Or Not: Fitting into the Cultural Mosaic*. "I feel like a real Canadian but am also proud to be Egyptian. Ironically, the very fact that I don't have to give up any part of my identity to become a real Canadian, increases my affection and feeling of belonging to my new country… Becoming a real Canadian did not require that I give up any part of who I was."[169]

Despite our many abject failures as a country, Canada has managed to establish a home where newcomers feel like they can belong. Novelist Irving Layton used to say, "A Canadian is someone who keeps asking the question, 'What is a Canadian?'"

Quebec, however, has a very different relationship with multiculturalism. When Prime Minister Pierre Trudeau introduced "a policy of multiculturalism within a bilingual framework," it was seen by Quebec as a threat to the survival of the French language and culture. By demoting French Quebec to just one cultural minority out of many, it felt like a federal ploy for the assimilation and disappearance of French Canada.

"Although there are two official languages, there is no official culture," Trudeau famously said. "Multiculturalism is commonly understood as an ideological program meant to drown or dilute Quebec's distinctiveness, to make it one more tile in the grand 'Canadian mosaic.' Emphasizing diversity over continuity would also erode Quebec's historical status of 'founder.'"[170]

The Quebec reaction has deep roots. Few francophones (inside or outside the province) forget Lord Durham's declarations about how best to unify Upper and Lower Canada during the rebellions of 1837-38.

---

169 Cherif Rifaat, *Immigrants Adapt, Countries Adopt. Or Not: Fitting into the Cultural* Mosaic (Toronto: New Canadians Press Incorporated, 2003), 26.

170 Geneviève Zubrzycki, *Beheading the Saint: Nationalism, Religion, And Secularism in Quebec* (Chicago: University of Chicago Press, 2016), 154.

"Durham was culturally biased against the French Canadians. He called them 'a people with no literature and no history.' He recommended assimilating them by uniting the Canadas in a way that would allow the English-speaking majority in Upper Canada to dominate."[171] Of course, among all this there was very little consideration for Indigenous communities. As the kids like to say, it's complicated.

When Pierre Elliot Trudeau patriated the Canadian Constitution in 1982 to replace the British North America Act, Quebec was the only province to not sign on. Subsequent attempts to woo it at Meech Lake (1987) and Charlottetown (1992) failed. Despite the impressive list of Quebec-born Canadian prime ministers and federal leaders who've helped shape Canadian politics and the country, the bitterness lingers. It's impossible to discuss Quebec's role within Canada without being reminded of the failed renegotiation of the province's status.

An interesting detail: while the failure of the Meech Lake Accord is seen mainly as a rejection of Quebec by Canada, it was just as much about the assertion of the rights of Indigenous peoples. When Elijah Harper, a Cree minister, withheld his signature, it spelled the real end of negotiations. A portent of what politics would come to look like: it would be unthinkable today to open up constitutional talks without Indigenous leaders at the table, yet that's exactly what happened then.[172]

---

171 David Mills, "The Durham Report," *The Canadian Encyclopedia*, February 6, 2006.

172 "25 Years since Elijah Harper said 'No' to the Meech Lake Accord," *CBC News*, June 11, 2015, https://www.cbc.ca/news/canada/ manitoba/25-years-since-elijah-harper-said-no-to-the-meech-lake-accord-1.3110439.

Constitutional failures aside, Quebec was officially granted status as a distinct society by the Royal Commission on Bilingualism and Biculturalism in 1963. Under the Conservative government of Stephen Harper, the Canadian House of Commons overwhelmingly passed a motion in 2006, recognizing that "the Québécois form a nation within a united Canada." While these declarations may be without constitutional force, federal concessions acknowledging Quebec's unique linguistic and cultural status are routinely allowed, most notably concerning immigration policy.

Quebec sets its own immigration policies, primarily with regard to the economic category and skilled workers, and understandably favours French-speaking applicants. While many Quebecers point out that federal interventions persist, Canada's input is limited enough that other provinces and territories have said that they, too, want less federal control over their immigration. The push and pull between provincial and federal jurisdictions continues, but often what is painted as outright rejection of Quebec is nothing more than territorial squabbling between a bunch of very different provinces and territories held together by a superglue of codependency, mistrust, indifference, grudging loyalty and, dare I say, occasionally even love. Like I said, it's complicated.

Unlike Canada's focus on multiculturalism, where a variety of cultures and practices coexist, Quebec prefers to emulate France's long-standing *laïcité* model of integration and interculturalism. Its supporters claim that by promoting one majority culture and language, it is easier for the various ethnic groups to find their way. A lack of exposure to majority values and customs, it is feared, will enable newcomers to cling to backward cultural traditions. In this view, multiculturalism is an obstacle to true social harmony and cohesion, preventing real integration and the acquisition of French as the common language.

In the rest of Canada, concerns about multiculturalism and diversity tend to be brought up by Conservative politicians. After Prime Minister Trudeau gave a speech in which he reiterated one of his favourite statements about "diversity being what makes Canada strong," Conservative MP Maxime Bernier (who would later found his own, far-more-right People's Party of Canada) went on a Trump-like Twitter rant about diversity.

"If anything and everything is Canadian, does being Canadian mean something?" he tweeted. "Shouldn't we emphasize our cultural traditions, what we have built and have in common, what makes us different from other cultures and societies?"

He continued: "Having people live among us who reject basic Western values such as freedom, equality, tolerance and openness doesn't make us strong." [173]

Without stipulating who these people were, he used inflammatory buzzwords like "ghetto," "extreme multiculturalism," "little tribes," and "cultural balkanization." He later clarified that it wasn't diversity that he had an issue with, but "ever more diversity." What does that even mean?

Erin Tolley, political science professor at the University of Toronto and author of *Framed: Media &*

---

173 Toula Drimonis, "Why You Should Worry When Maxime Bernier Loses his Marbles Over Canadian Diversity," *National Observer*, August 15, 2018.

the Coverage of Race in Canadian Politics, responded to Bernier's thread on Twitter, brilliantly debunking many of his arguments. This included pointing out the rather awkward fact that when Bernier decided to throw around words like tribes to describe homogenous groups, he forgot that Beauce, the Quebec riding he represents, is almost 99 percent francophone and white. But I guess those cultural and linguistic "ghettoes" don't count.

Interculturalism is described as a policy that respects differences, but doesn't celebrate them, so as to not deepen the divide. What professor Michel Seymour describes as a relationship of "reciprocal recognition."[174] Like multiculturalism, interculturalism is a policy of cultural pluralism that favours integration, not assimilation, but ensures that the common language is French.

Based on its main defining points, Quebec's official policy of interculturalism isn't all that different from multiculturalism. It, too, encourages diversity, pluralism, and communication—as long as it's in French. Interculturalism simply refuses to place an emphasis on what writer Akos Verboczy refers to as "the glorification of differences."

So, where does this leave Quebec allophones like myself? Awkwardly stuck in the middle, as usual. Most Quebec allophones and new immigrants have neither a past grievance with a British colonial state nor a deeply embedded mistrust of multiculturalism. On the contrary, there is nothing more anathema to multilingual allophones such as myself than state-enforced homogeneity and policy that suggests that you're failing as a

---

174 Michel Seymour, *Raison, Déraison, et Religion: Plaidoyer pour une laïcité ouverte* (Montreal: Écosociété, 2021).

Quebecer if you continue speaking your first language at home and English with your friends, and if you don't remove your hijab and hide your religion.

Most allophones gravitate towards multiculturalism not because, as many Quebec nationalists insist, they always vote for federalist parties like a mindless monolith or because they were brainwashed by successive federal governments. They do it because multiculturalism doesn't demand that allophones cede parts of who they are in order to be accepted by the whole. It's as simple as that.

Quebec's need to police differences exhausts allophones because it is seen as a betrayal of the desire to maintain our first languages and cultures. Heterogeneity is problematic, and visible cultural and religious diversity becomes a national crisis.

An additional problem with legislating homogeneity is that people acquire an aversion to differences, promoting a noticeable increase in projection bias. Projection bias is the belief that others automatically share the same attitudes and beliefs that we do. So, the more something is normalized for the majority, the more the majority believes that *this is just how it's supposed to be.*

Nuance is important here. Inasmuch as uniformity can lay the groundwork for intolerance, a society like Quebec that prioritizes uniformity isn't de facto intolerant. But, when you normalize or legislate expectations of sameness, you give carte blanche to racists to discriminate against the *other.* It's not that consensus doesn't have its value, it's just that the trade-off is questionable when it comes to entire societies, especially in today's diverse, multilingual, multifaith world.

As Shakil Choudhury says, "Most people are taught the Golden Rule: Treat people as you want to be treated. In equity work this has been modified to become one step more inclusive. Known as the Platinum Rule, it is to treat people *as they want to be treated*."[175]

Quebec has veered considerably from its original interpretation of interculturalism. In 2017, when I was asked to write a foreword for the English translation of Akos Verboczy's book, *Rhapsody in Quebec: On the Path of an Immigrant Child*, I wrote: "There are as many ways to be a Quebecer as there are ways to love this place."[176]

I didn't know it at the time, but I was echoing Quebec premier and PQ leader René Lévesque's words when he rejected federal multiculturalism and introduced his own version of interculturalism in 1981. "In its place, the government of Quebec proposed a policy of cultural convergence. The policy was entitled 'Many ways of being a Quebecer.' Its principal objective was to 'ensure the maintenance and development of cultural communities and their specificities, make French-speaking Quebecers aware of the contribution of cultural communities to our common heritage and finally promote the integration of cultural communities in Quebec society and especially in sectors where they are particularly underrepresented."[177]

Where did that vision of interculturalism go?

175 Shakil Choudhury, *Deep Diversity: Overcoming Us vs. Them* (Toronto: Between the Lines, 2015), 178.

176 Akos Verboczy, *Rhapsody in Quebec: On the Path of an Immigrant Child*, trans. Casey Roberts (Montreal: Baraka Books, 2017).

177 Jack Jedwab, "Multiculturalism," *The Canadian Encyclopedia*, March 20, 2020.

Since its election in 2018, the CAQ has worked hard to play up a need for "social cohesion" by promoting a uniform national agenda and an extremely limited and singular identity that excludes minorities and diverging points of view. This insistence on a singular ethnocentric vision leaves the rest of us with only two options: we either remove all markers of our identity, or we remain excluded. Allophones, through no fault of our own, are the enemy, the ones who dilute French identity.

Speaking at the Ukrainian Canadian Congress in 1971, Prime Minister Pierre Trudeau said, "There are few policies potentially more disastrous for Canada than to tell all Canadians that they must be alike. There is no such thing as a model or ideal Canadian. What could be more absurd than the concept of an all-Canadian boy or girl? A society which emphasizes uniformity is one which creates intolerance and hate."[178]

---

178 Lia Grainger, "Pierre Elliott Trudeau Once Praised the Value of Diversity, Inclusiveness," *Yahoo! News*, November 22, 2016, https://ca.news.yahoo.com/pierre-elliot-trudeau-praised-the-value-of-diversity-inclusiveness-in-1971-223029284.html/.

20. Layers, Not Fractions

When people tell me who and what I am, implying that certain facets of my identity are more or less important or that how I define myself isn't accurate, it is exasperating. It doesn't matter where the order, accusation, or guilt trip is coming from.

You're a Canadian first. You're a Quebecer first. You're Greek first.

No. I'm all those things at once. I'm each of them separately and sequentially. I am any of them at any given time. Does speaking English diminish my ability to speak Greek or love French? Does my love of Greece alter in any possible way my affinity for Quebec? Does celebrating Quebec's *Fête nationale* stop me from celebrating Greek Independence Day or Canada Day? If I had three kids, would people insist I choose one as my favourite?

In *"Qui ça, nous?"* (Who's that, us?), Quebec journalist Noémi Mercier writes about what we lose and what we gain when we discuss collective identities in our society. She acknowledges that appeals to a collective identity can be extremely beneficial (particularly in pandemic times, which is when it was written) for our physical and mental health, self-esteem and motivation, as well as our need for meaning and social cohesion.

However, she continues, "When I hear an elected official, an artist, a commentator say 'we,' I imagine him drawing a big circle around himself, as if he defined a playground with a stick in the sand, and I wonder which of us it embraces in its radius, and who it discards. Because the 'we' is more than a cocoon, it's a border; it excludes at the same time as it circumscribes. There are tangible consequences for those we keep out."[179]

Her beautifully written piece is an astute examination of the real damage that nationalism, tribal instincts, and xenophobia can inflict. However, it's also hopeful because she points to some great examples of how people can be taught to form new alliances and new connections that focus on their humanity and override deeply rooted racial bias or ethno-nationalism. She reminds us that these psychological barriers are arbitrary creations, and therefore subject to change. Isn't that what immigration and acceptance of the *other* is, after all?

"We are not rigid, one-dimensional beings," she concludes.

> Each of us contains a multitude of identities, a panoply of 'selves' who belong to different social groups. At some point I can identify myself as a woman first; the next minute, I'll define myself as a Montrealer or a journalist. I can imagine myself as the descendant of a line of French-Canadians as well as the daughter of a Haitian immigrant. And depending on whether I wake up in one or another of these versions of myself, I can feel my

---

179 Noémi Mercier, "Qui ça, nous?" *L'Actualité*, June 2, 2020.

solidarities move, encompass different categories of humans, contract or expand inside me.

For some, a new life is a chance at new choices. Part of a successful adaptation is when the place of their birth, culture, or language evolves from primary identity to one of many. For some, it's a complete renouncement of their past identity and an embrace of the new one only. And that's entirely fine! That's their decision to make. Not long ago, Magdalena Michalowska, a Polish immigrant to Quebec, posted to Facebook that she wanted nothing to do with being an immigrant or a Polish Quebecer.

"Choosing to immigrate is to renounce carrying your country with you," she wrote. "I didn't deny it, I grew. I adapted. I'm not a ghetto-like statistic, I'm not a performance object, I'm not distinct, I'm not unique, I'm not diversity. Even if they want to reduce me to my qualities as an immigrant, I've become a Quebecer and I always will be."

Magdalena's declaration is every bit as valid as someone else's choice to hold on to their heritage as part of their identity. Immigrants might share reference points, values, and preferences, but we all have different responses to picking up and starting a new life. None of those responses necessarily predict who will be a better majority member.

New York-based educator and writer Kim Katrin Milan shared a quote from singer and voice teacher Yumi Tomsha on Instagram, which I found so lovely: "I am not 'half Japanese' and 'half Lithuanian Jewish.'" When I'm singing a Japanese folk song, I don't sing with half my voice, but with my whole voice. When I'm taping together my grandparents' Jewish marriage contract, worn by time but still resilient, it's not half of my heart that is moved but my whole heart. I am complete, and I embody layers of identities that belong together. I am made of layers, not fractions."

Layers, not fractions.

Every day I wake up and embrace all of it. Not *part* of it. Not one part to the *detriment* of the other. Not one part *instead* of another. It's layers upon layers of identity, like the soft layers of fabric that add warmth and texture to a quilt, layers you can't possibly tug at without unravelling all the interconnected stitches that make you *you*. I can't separate and compartmentalize the ingredients and elements that I'm made of without radically altering the final version. Why would I want to?

I'm a Quebecer, I'm Greek, I'm Canadian… I'm all of those things. I don't know where one identity ends and another begins. Once you've been raised to have all these parts of you feel like home, they all belong to you and you belong to all of them.

Additions, not subtractions.

Layers, not fractions.

They're all mine. I'm not giving anything back.

21. Speaking Out

French Quebecers who study in English, or who travel, work, and vacation abroad don't magically transform into anglophones or Brits or Spaniards or Floridians. Identity doesn't dissipate into nothingness at the first border crossing, but neither is it a delicate orchid needing protection in a cultural greenhouse. A healthy culture should be able to withstand the pull of everything around it.

Former Quebec premier Jacques Parizeau studied at the London School of Economics and was a well-known anglophile. Current PQ leader Paul St-Pierre Plamondon studied at McGill and Oxford. Former Quebec premier Robert Bourassa studied at both Oxford and Harvard universities, yet is responsible for Bill 22, the precursor to Bill 101, which declared French to be the sole official language of the province. Lucien Bouchard believed in English private education for his sons, yet remained a nationalist his entire political career, going as far as founding the Bloc Québécois. Somehow, they all managed not only to resist English assimilation but many went on to become leaders of the effort to win Quebec independence.

Why have so many political leaders in Quebec managed to enjoy and benefit from English institutions, international studies, and knowledge of multiple languages, while not trusting that the average Quebecer can do the same? Why don't they have more faith in the *hoi polloi* (Greek, meaning "the masses")? Why isn't the focus more on government investments where it actually makes a difference: education and promotion of language and culture?

When allophones and English speakers do exactly what French speakers are doing—fighting to retain their language and culture—they are seen by some as traitors, as the spoke in the wheel, the "money and the ethnic vote" guilty of preventing Quebec from becoming a country.[180] Language purists believe that you can welcome immigrants to increase an anemic birth rate, yet still assure a society that is culturally and linguistically homogeneous—even inside private homes. That's an irrational and impossible ask.

It's also deeply unfair. The allophones and anglophones that I know are proud of and attached to Quebec. Many of us identify as Quebecers first, and Canadians second. We take pride in speaking French and consider it both an asset and a big part of our identity. We rally to defend the province when away and enjoy pointing out what Quebec has done better than the rest of Canada. This is our home, too, and we shouldn't have to spend our days explaining this irrefutable and non-negotiable fact to random strangers who feel entitled to demand proof of our loyalty and our "Quebecitude" simply because their last name is Tremblay or their ancestors arrived here a few decades before ours.

---

180 "Parizeau Blames 'Money and the Ethnic Vote' for Referendum Loss," *CBC Archives*, October 30, 1995.

Even Quebec's crankiest and harshest critic, novelist Mordecai Richler, reviled by *indépendantistes* for his often caustic takedowns of his home province, unequivocally stated that he could not live anywhere else in Canada. "So far as one can generalize, the most gracious, cultivated, and innovative people in this country are French Canadians. Certainly, they have given us the most exciting politicians of our time: Trudeau, Lévesque. Without them, Canada would be an exceedingly boring and greatly diminished place."[181]

That doesn't sound like someone who hated Quebec. It sounds like someone who had a different political and social vision (and he was certainly entitled to it) as are the French Quebecers who are staunch federalists and proud Canadians.

For those who dream of a single-minded version of Quebec that demands assimilation at all costs, the struggle continues. They may have a generation of ethnic kids who speak impeccable French, but many of those kids remain lukewarm to the idea of an independent Quebec. The assimilationists want more Ruba Ghazal and Maka Kotto, two immigrant Quebec politicians who support Quebec independence, and less Sugar Sammy and Liberal MNA Marwah Rizqy, who are staunch federalists.

Samir Khullar is the poster child for Bill 101. Better known by his stage name Sugar Sammy, a Montreal-born son of Indian immigrants, grew up in Côte-des-Neiges, one of Montreal's most diverse neighbourhoods. He spoke Hindi and Punjabi at home, English because he watched English TV, and French in elementary and

181 Mordecai Richler, *Oh Canada, Oh Quebec: Requiem for a Divided Country* (Toronto: Penguin Books, 1992), 260.

high school. With a deep understanding of Quebec identity and language issues, he's perfectly equipped to practise his brand of acerbic comedy in both languages, and has built a career offending nationalists.

"I speak four languages and don't think about it much," he said on Quebec AM, a radio show on *CBC*, a few years back. "It's just part of my identity and who I am. Some hardliners believe that if you don't believe exactly what they believe in, especially as a public figure with some influence, then it's treason. That's a dangerous way to look at things."

In 2012, he came up with the idea of a bilingual show, "You're Gonna *Rire*." It played to his strengths as a home-grown allophone comfortable in multiple cultures. He doesn't shy away from snarky quips and pokes holes in arguments about identity politics. If he pushes buttons, it's because he knows that he can. Suffice it to say, he's made some enemies along the way.

"Humour allows you to address taboos," he said in an interview with Dan Bilefsky for *The New York Times*. "In Quebec, the ultimate taboo is identity."[182]

"If Sugar Sammy is the future of Quebec, then Quebec has no future," wrote *Journal de Montréal* columnist and chronic overreactor Mathieu Bock-Côté.[183] The truth is that Sugar Sammy and other children of immigrants like him *are* the future of Quebec. The province and the French language won't survive otherwise.

---

182 Dan Bilefsky, "A Quebec Comedian is Happy to Offend in any Language," *The New York Times*, August 11, 2018.

183 Mathieu Bock-Côté, "Le Québec de Sugar Sammy," *Le Journal de Montréal*, May 14, 2013.

As a Quebec allophone, Sugar Sammy's political awakening came after the 1995 referendum for Quebec independence failed by a razor-thin margin, followed by then-Premier Jacques Parizeau's angry concession speech blaming the loss on "money and the ethnic vote."

"The comments stung Mr. Khullar, who was 19. 'Here I was a teenager who was doing everything to be part of Quebec society and I was being told that I was responsible for the failure of Quebec's dream of statehood,' he recalled. 'I realized that I would always be 'the other' in Quebec, no matter what language I spoke.'"[184]

Parizeau's unfortunate and divisive comments have been cited as the reason many Quebec allophones and anglophones, to this day, will never be tempted by the independence movement. It was an ungracious thing to say, and most importantly, inaccurate. To blame the loss on Quebec's ethnic communities and federal money was to conveniently ignore the 40 percent of francophones who also voted in favour of staying in Canada.

Rosa Pires, a Quebecer of Portuguese origins, whose parents, out of loyalty to the separatist movement, put her in French school before Bill 101 even came into law, grew up supporting the separatist movement and the PQ. But she, too, was disillusioned by Parizeau's deeply divisive comments.

In *Ne Sommes-Nous Pas Québécoises?* (Aren't we Quebecers?) Pires talks about how she never felt represented by Quebec's all-white feminism that failed to appreciate the challenges faced by immigrant and second-generation women, and who demanded

---

184 Dan Bilefsky, "A Quebec Comedian is Happy to Offend in any Language."

assimilation and rejection of immigrants' multiple identities in order to belong to Quebec society. [185]

Francis Boucher wrote an equally perceptive book
about those who felt excluded from the dream of Quebec
independence. In *La Grande Déception*, he explored how
the PQ's Charter of Values alienated many members of
the province's ethnic and Indigenous communities. [186]

Boucher cites "Speak What" by Italian-Quebec playwright and poet Marco Micone, a French-language
poem written in 1989 that made direct and bitter reference to Michèle Lalonde's famous poem "Speak White."
Written and performed in 1968, Lalonde's poem used a
taunt that English-speaking bosses would hurl at French
Quebecers who couldn't—or wouldn't—speak English:
"Speak white!"

"Speak White" was an anthemic manifesto in defiance
of English colonialism and a system that disadvantaged
and oppressed Quebec francophones.[187] There is not a
Quebec separatist alive who does not know that poem at
least partly by heart. But thirty years or so after the Quiet
Revolution, Micone wrote a retort that pointed the finger back at Quebecers, accusing them of now oppressing
other minorities, primarily immigrants.

> Speak what
>
> Comment parlez-vous
>
> Dans vos salons huppés

185 Rosa Pires, *Ne Sommes-Nous Pas Québécoises* (Montréal: Éditions du remue-ménage, 2019).
186 Francis Boucher, *La Grande Déception* (Montréal: Éditions Somme toute, 2018), 22.
187 Michèle Lalonde, *Speak White* (Montréal: Les Éditions de L'Hexagone, 1974).

Vous souvenez-vous du vacarme des usines
and of the voice des contremaîtres
you sound like them more and more.

(Speak what
How do you speak
In your posh living rooms
Do you remember the din of the factories
and the voice of the foremen?
You sound like them more and more.)[188]

The poem replicates the same accusatory and bitter tone of the original, written by someone who, like Pires, was once a supporter of the independence movement. "Is he right?" asks Boucher. "Have we become the foreman, the little bosses, now?"

A proud Quebecer and defender of the French language, Micone, who arrived here from Italy at the age of thirteen, rejects Legault's ethnic nationalism and identity politics. Interviewed by *Le Devoir* in 2021 for his new book, *On ne naît pas Québécois, on le devient* (One is not born Québécois, one becomes it), he urged francophones not to fall for the CAQ's "stunted and petty nationalism."

"I tell francophones not to repeat the dominant-dominated relationship they suffered with anglophones at immigrants' expense," he says. "The minority status of Quebecers is a double-edged sword: uncertainty can have unfortunate consequences, but there is also the possibility of showing solidarity with other minorities."[189]

---

188 Marco Micone, *Speak What* (Montréal: VLB éditeur, 2001, 1989), 14.
189 Dominic Tardif, "Pour l'amour du Québec," *Le Devoir,* July 3, 2021.

If the Quebec sovereigntist movement had allowed for more plurality, complexity, and diversity, I suspect it would have had a better chance of gaining support among ethnically diverse communities. While some current nationalist parties do, indeed, have progressive and inclusive elements, I think that ship has sailed. Support for Quebec independence has lost considerable steam since the 1995 referendum, with a 2020 Leger poll showing only 36 percent support for the movement. That number drops to 26 percent among young Quebecers aged eighteen to twenty-four. "Right now, the movement is dormant," said political analyst Karim Boulos. "If you're waiting for the youth to revive it, you'll be waiting a long time."[190] A 2020 Angus Reid poll asking Canadians how satisfied they were with the direction Canada was headed revealed that 76 percent of Quebecers were happy.[191] Those are not numbers that suggest any real and current appetite for Quebec independence. As demographics continue to change, Quebec's nationalist movement has often responded with ever more exclusionary talk, engaging in a vicious cycle of recrimination.

In this increasingly multicultural and multilingual world, it is almost impossible to define a singular Québécois identity. Many Quebecers' desire for one is literally unsustainable.

When former Quebec Premier Jacques Parizeau died in 2015, I wrote a sympathetic editorial contextualizing

---

190 Tina Tenneriello, Kelsey Patterson, "How Would Quebec's Separatist Movement Fare in a Referendum Today?" *CityNews Montreal*, October 28, 2020.

191 Stuart Thomson, "How Satisfied are You with Things in Canada? Poll Reveals a Chasm Between Alberta, Quebec," *The National Post*, January 15, 2020.

his 1995 "money and the ethnic vote" outburst. In response, I was lambasted by English speakers as an "ass-kisser" and "a naïve little girl who didn't know her history." I don't think I've gotten that much hate mail ever for a single editorial I've written in my entire career, so when francophones call me a Rhodesian, I can't help but laugh.[192]

After it went viral, some francophones saw me as a friendly ally, a pleasant exception to the rule. I was invited by talk show host Christiane Charrette to sit on a TV panel with producer and host Guy A. Lepage, director and actor Serge Denoncourt, and former Parti Québécois leader Jean-François Lisée, among others, on *125, Marie-Anne*.[193] Everyone—including Lisée, who had been Parizeau's speechwriter that fateful evening—conceded that the comment had been uncalled for; he referred to it as "committing political suicide." Lisée reminded us he had written a concession speech that an emotional (and perhaps slightly tipsy) Parizeau opted to reject. He instead went rogue and spoke without notes. The speech was lambasted in the Canadian and international press for being ethnocentric and many in the *Oui* camp were surprised, insulted, and angered. Even fellow PQ member Bernard Landry said that the movement had to "hide its head in shame."[194]

I would later be interviewed by *Le Devoir*. Journalist Marco Fortier and I sat on the grass by the Lachine Canal on a gorgeous June day and had a lengthy and

---

192 Toula Drimonis, "Can We Get Over Jacques Parizeau's 'Money and Ethnic Vote' Comment Already," *HeadSpace*, June 2, 2015.

193 "125, rue Marie-Anne," *Télé-Québec*, June 5, 2015.

194 Mario Cardinal, *Breaking Point Quebec—Canada: The 1995 Referendum* (Montreal: Bayard Canada Livres, 2005), 410.

affable conversation, where I explained my attachment to Quebec and why I thought life here was far more pleasant than certain pundits would have us believe.

C'est toujours rentable pour les médias de donner la parole aux grandes gueules et aux extrémistes. La réalité est pas mal plus ennuyeuse: la réalité, c'est que la vie est belle au Québec," dit-elle dans un français impeccable.

(It's always much more profitable for the media to give a platform to loudmouths and extremists. Reality is much more boring: the reality is that life is good in Quebec,' she says in impeccable French.)

Years later, I stand by that statement, although my French is far from impeccable.

I went home from *125, Marie-Anne* that night to hundreds of new Twitter followers —all of them francophones—grateful for the olive branch and the attempt at understanding. I would later join popular French-language current affairs show, *Bazzo TV*, hosted by well-known Quebec journalist Marie-France Bazzo, as one of their rotating political panelists for the show's final season.

This has happened often in my career. French Quebecers are so thirsty for what they love and value to be recognized and appreciated by others that they routinely respond with genuine gratitude and joy. In 2019-20 I was one of the panelists on MAtv's French television cultural show *Nous sommes la ville*, created and hosted by French journalist Marilyse Hamelin. The show was 100 percent Montreal, and boasted the kind of diversity that is still a rarity on mainstream Quebec television.

My job was to discuss two Quebec literary works during each appearance. For a bookworm such as myself, this was a dream come true. The vast majority of books I recommended were French, with the occasional English title or translation, but always with a focus on Quebec. I loved having the opportunity to introduce viewers of all languages to these literary offerings and enjoyed showing francophones that anglophones and allophones were also interested in Quebec culture and local authors.

I can't tell you the number of times I was stopped in public by viewers eager to tell me how much they appreciated my love for Quebec culture. It continues to surprise me that they're so genuinely shocked.

When I see how Quebec francophones are perceived by many in the rest of Canada, the unflattering misconceptions and the vitriol, I can understand why. Many in the ROC neither understand nor care how gripped by insecurity, how cornered francophones often feel. Every slip in the demographics, every indication that French is losing ground, every arrogant and dismissive taunt by Canadian anglophones who can't possibly relate, pushes buttons that are incredibly easy to push.

As a result, and as collateral damage in this constant tension, Quebec's anglophones and allophones are lumped in with English-speaking Canadians from outside Quebec and often bear the brunt of this animosity. In addition, many francophones continue to experience English as the language of domination, even though statistics show Quebec's anglophones currently have a much bleaker socio-economic reality than francophones in the province.

Predictably, the love fest after my appearance on *125, Marie-Anne* didn't last long. The following week, I wrote a somewhat sarcastic defence of Montreal actor

Jay Baruchel for the *National Post*. He had been vilified by no fewer than six (!) francophone pundits for committing the "offence" of admitting that linguistic tension had partially motivated his decision to move to Toronto from his hometown, Montreal. How dare Baruchel say out loud what every single exasperated allophone and anglophone (and more than one francophone) in this province has thought of at least once in their lives. Immediately, the hate started rolling in, accusing me of Quebec bashing.

A few years later, while in Greece in 2018, I found myself sitting on a deserted beach in the town of Monemvasia, absorbed in a book I had picked up during one of my routine visits to Montreal's used bookstores. *Boundaries of Identity: A Quebec Reader* is a little-known but fascinating collection of essays, interviews, manifestos, and newspaper articles written by some of Quebec's most well-known intellectuals, writers, and journalists, among them Dorothy Williams, Yves Beauchemin, Charles Taylor, Anne Hébert, and Jean-François Lisée, who was a working journalist at the time. Published in 1992, the book had long been out of print and it immediately caught my attention.

It was on this beach in southern Greece that I came to read what adamant separatist Pierre Vallières wrote in *Le Devoir* in 1990:

> Our politicians, driven by the urgency of gaining the maximum advantage from the nationalist momentum, have forgotten that pluralistic debate is the necessary condition for all democratic practice... To build a society, a truly free country, we

must move away from a performance democracy, a showbiz democracy, towards a democracy of participation that is pluralistic and creative, where no one will be left out in the cold.[195]

Those who get left out in the cold won't be inclined to support the house that shuts the door on them. Ignoring the fact that Quebec never was and never will be a monolithic society is to fight for a mythologized past and an imaginary future. Letting someone into your world, in the form of immigration, doesn't mean you get to define who they become. We need *all* voices and *all* perspectives to be heard. It doesn't even matter whether we define ourselves as federalists or sovereigntists; francophones, anglophones, or allophones. What matters is that we all be able to define ourselves as Quebecers. But, in order to do that, we must first feel accepted.

---

195 William Dodge, ed., transl. Christopher Korchin, *Boundaries of Identity: A Quebec Reader* (Toronto: Lester Publishing Limited, 1992), 44.

22. Who Are the Others?

It is not our purpose to become each other;
it is to recognize each other, to learn to see the
other and honour him for what he is.

—Hermann Hesse

I woke up this morning from a dream where I was ten years old and visiting my dad's village in Greece. My brother and I were running like banshees through the mountain trails behind the patrimonial home. Our legs brushed up against the wild thyme, myrtles, prickly burnet and oregano, and the air burst with intoxicating aromas. I was tanned from the sun, my legs covered in dusty ochre-coloured dirt, my hands sticky from sampling perfectly ripe late-summer figs, and the cicadas were playing that unbroken song I always associate with August.

I was ten. I was in Greece. I had endless time and space to roam, my grandparents and my dad were still alive, and I was not yet marked by life's losses. It was a good dream.

Later that day I was in a taxi. The driver, a beautiful dreadlocked Haitian man blasting classical music from his radio, told me it looked like it was going to rain. At the red light, three giggling schoolgirls wearing multicoloured hijabs crossed the street. An Asian teenager with bright purple hair glanced up at us from her book, saw nothing of interest, and returned to reading. A gaggle of teenage girls were gathering outside École Polyvalente Saint-Henri. I saw beautiful big Afros and Doc Martens, braces, short skirts, manicured fingernails with chipped burgundy polish, kids holding books they just couldn't wait to put aside for the summer. I heard *"Ben voyons…t'es folle!"* from their mouths and Coeur de pirate and Koriass from their iPhones. They looked like they were from all over. But they belonged to Quebec. You could tell from their accents and the ease with which they navigated their bodies, feet firmly planted on the sidewalk, STM metro cards in their hands, ready to disperse to their homes in various corners of the city.

That night, I was at home reading excerpts from *Immigrec*, a university project documenting the experiences of Greek-Canadian immigrants. I came across an interview with Mrs. Eleni Manoli-Tsakalis, from Elassona in Greece, now resident of Toronto. I recognized the name of her hometown. It's not that far from where my parents were from.

"I go to Greece, I miss Canada, I come to Canada, I miss Greece. I have two cultures. I want the culture of Greece, I want the Canadian, too. I want to celebrate Thanksgiving, I want to celebrate on the 24th of June when Saint-Jean-Baptiste celebrates, and I want to celebrate the 1st of July when Canada celebrates. I also celebrate without a doubt on the 25th of March in the [Greek] parade. We've gone out even with 27C below zero in the parade. Aren't we going to parade? That is two loves in one heart. That's what I'm telling you."

Later that weekend I was at a Montreal wedding where the bride gave a speech in Vietnamese for her parents, switched to French to address her brothers, spoke English while joking around with guests, and then managed some Punjabi to address her new husband's family. No one thought anything of it. This is our *normal*.

Then it was the tail end of winter 2020 (just weeks before COVID-19 hit) and I was in Gaspésie skiing and snowshoeing. The last time I was here I was in my early twenties, camping and hiking Parc Forillon with a boyfriend who would later become my husband and then my ex. He didn't (and I suspect still doesn't) like hiking, but I wanted to go and so we did. Looking back on it, I cringe that I insisted he do something he didn't want to. It's confirmation that I have grown up.

At one point, I found myself alone on the trail, snowshoeing that very same stretch along the waterfront that we took years ago. Decades later, I recognized the homes and the shimmering, soft slope of the curve as I descended the path. The snow crunched underneath my feet and transcendent whiteness bounced off the ground. It felt like a luminous homecoming. "Welcome back," I heard the forest whisper.

At night my hiking group shared stories of blisters and aches, tips to prevent more blisters and aches. We sang old French songs, drank wine, and sampled maple-syrup mille-feuilles at the Gîte du Mont-Albert. Collin was a British journalist from the UK writing a piece for *The Guardian*. He called the Chic-Chocs "Chick-Chocks" and no one had the heart to correct him. Pierre was an archeologist who spent summers in digs in Syria and Greece. He told me how he saw the ruins in

Aleppo before they were destroyed first by the Taliban then by the Russians. Diane was a land surveyor who traveled throughout Quebec, used to attending meetings where one person spoke French, the other replied in English, and a third in Cree. François was a farmer from Drummondville whose lean, weather-beaten face and callused hands remind me of my Greek uncles who also spent a lifetime working the land. Wrinkles so deep the sun can't reach them anymore. It was his sixth time attending *Les traversées de la Gaspésie*. Over seafood lasagna and sugar pie we talked about history, religion, and Indigenous rights. My preconceived notions about what a seventy-year-old French Quebec farmer would be interested in were joyfully debunked.

Claudine, the organizer, was a spry older woman with the energy of someone in their thirties. She believed that the more you sleep, the less fun you have. She nicknamed me *ma p'tite toutou* (my little teddy bear). She ran around making sure everything went smoothly, yelling out, "Enjoy-*ez vous*!" and toasting À la vie qui nous *unit* when she raised her glass. To life that unites us!

I once lived in a place where everyone I knew and interacted with was Greek. It was lovely and it was fine, but this version of "lovely and fine" is even more magical and alive.

AFTERWORD

I wrote this book with no map, but I always knew the destination.

So much of what second- and third-generation immigrants experience is unique and either left unsaid or shared in jest, leaving us isolated and lonely. As an allophone living in Quebec, I no longer care about what anglophones and francophones think of each other. The constant *one-upping*, the Misery Olympics about who has suffered more. I'm so over the collective gaslighting, the accusatory back-and-forth between two of the country's colonizing forces that keeps us from moving forward on important issues, and reaching our full potential.

While there are legitimate concerns from both communities, no one has better expressed the frustration of constantly exaggerated grievances from Quebec's two main linguistic groups than the late Liberal MNA Reed Scowen. During his farewell speech to the National Assembly, he said: "If I follow the reasoning of both sides to its logical conclusion, in two generations there won't be a single anglophone left in Quebec, but everybody will be speaking English."

In a *Canadaland* podcast episode with Jesse Brown, opinion columnist Emilie Nicolas accurately summarized how minority groups often feel. "The way Canadian media plays out, it's an endless hockey game between the Canadien Habs and the Toronto Maple Leafs, and people of colour are basically the puck, we're not even players, we are the puck. And it's just two different kinds of white people trying to argue who is the best and personally I'm not interested in that kind of debate."

Neither am I.

The boring, uneventful reality that most pundits won't bother writing about is that, for the most part, we all get along just fine. Quebec is a wonderful place to live and people of all linguistic backgrounds treat each other with respect, affection, and kindness. Don't let inflammatory headlines and Twitter fights fool you. A simple walk around the neighbourhood will remind you otherwise. This is a beautiful place to call home.

This book is a tribute to my parents and to every first generation of immigrants. The aunts and uncles who worked hard and then laughed harder, playing cards and drinking wine while I fell asleep on a pile of coats in the bedroom. The generation who let their Greek-Canadian kids listen to American Top-40, and bike to the dep to stack up on *Tiger Beat* and *Archie* comics, but who also insisted they speak their language, memorize the Battle of Marathon, and be taught how to make spanakopita. Multiple worlds were going to be crammed into our little bodies, there would be no negotiation.

This book is a grateful *thank you* to everyone who has packed their bags and their dreams and travelled to a new place they hoped would make room for both. I wanted to share what it feels like to be an immigrant's daughter, someone who feels every bit a part of this place, but is also acutely aware of the sacrifices, the discrimination, the lucky chances, the longing, and the conflicted loyalties newcomers face.

This is the kind of book that has no real ending. Immigration doesn't stop. Human migration will continue as long as there is life on the planet. It can be hindered, it can be legislated to a crawl, it can be temporarily restricted. But it will continue. With the climate crisis amplifying, it's only expected to increase, and not for the best of reasons.

The stories we tell about ourselves, our cultures, our languages, and our homes are our life preservers. They carry us to safety on dry land. When we're unsure, they lend us identity and a sense of recognition. "That's who I am!" we cry out.

What if our world simply expanded to include more? What if, as James Baldwin said, "we create ourselves, without finding it necessary to create an enemy"?[196]

What if we just start seeing everything around us as *our* culture, *our* country, *our* home, *our* values? Would you recognize yourself there?

People exactly *like you* go somewhere else and people *nothing like you* arrive. With a little trust and time, you eventually realize there are no *others*. It's always been just *us*.

---

196 Eddie S. Glaude Jr., *Begin Again: James Baldwin's America and Its Urgent Lessons for Our Own* (New York: Crown, 2020), 90.

Acknowledgements

The idea for this book began percolating after my dad passed away in 2013. I became increasingly nostalgic for a time when he was still walking this earth and wanted to pay tribute to his life—and the lives of those with similar trajectories. As both his daughter and a writer, I had the ability and opportunity to voice what immigration is all about, both personally and politically. I wanted to do this for the first and second generations, and for everyone who has ever felt like an *other* at one point in their lives. I only wish he was here to see the final product.

The "shitty first draft" (what writer Anne Lamott refers to in *Bird by Bird* as the initial and necessary spewing of words without any thought to structure) first occurred over two years ago. It subsequently took many revisions (most of the work done in the middle of a pandemic) to narrow it down to what you're now holding in your hands. As cliché-ridden as the expression is, this has truly been a labour of love for me.

Immense gratitude to my family. My loud, expressive, overdramatic, cacophonous, loving, occasionally suffocating, always supportive Greek family. You occasionally drive me nuts, but I don't know who I'd be without you. Probably a calmer, far less interesting person. Dad, mom, Terry, Dee, Nia, Richard, Panayote, I love you. Σας αγαπώ.

Thank you to my extended family, both here in Montreal and back in Greece, for having my back, reminding me of my roots, and always making me laugh.

To the team at Linda Leith Publishing for taking a chance at a long-time columnist, first-time author with a penchant for repetition, thank you. Sincere gratitude to Linda Leith, Leila Marshy, and Elise Moser for treating my firstborn with the care and love it needed and for refusing to let me drop it on its head. I am grateful for your patience, guidance, meticulous attention to detail, and the respect with which you treated something that was so personal and precious to me.

Thank you to all the friends and lovers who have ever said, "You should write a book." My gratitude remains. Thank you to my close friends who offered an ear and a shoulder when the process was too long and too frustrating. There are so many of you and I recognize how lucky I am to have you in my life. Adriana, extra gratitude to you, for being this book's first reader and first champion. *Mille grazie.*

Thank you to everyone who has ever read my byline as a long-time columnist with *TC Media, Ricochet Media, Daily Hive,* the *National Observer,* and *Cult MTL* over the years, offering precious feedback and reminding me that the topics I choose to tackle matter and resonate.

My deepest appreciation to those who agreed to read my manuscript before publication and blurb about it, often offering advice and feedback that only improved it: UQAM Professor and scientific director of Geopolitics at the Raoul Dandurand Chair, Élisabeth Vallet; the Honourable Romeo Saganash; the Honourable Marlene Jennings; the Honourable Eleni Bakopanos; journalist and columnist Fariha Naqvi Mohamed, and filmmaker Michael Fukushima. Thank you for your time and valuable insight. I am honoured you all said yes to my request.

My respect and gratitude to those who've written and reported extensively on immigration, government policies and identity politics. You provided guidance, insight, research, footnotes, and resources. There is a bibliography at the end of this book I would encourage everyone to explore.

As Quebec and Canada keep evolving, and as immigration changes our common landscape as well as the definitions that we use to describe one another, I fully anticipate that there will be new generations of bilingual and trilingual Quebecers for whom the terms francophone, anglophone, and allophone may no longer apply. For many multilingual Quebecers and Canadians, such singular definitions already feel too limiting and reductionist. For the moment, they remain adequate and are the definitions most of my research and news articles are based on. As such, for the purposes of this book, I remain an allophone.

No matter your ethnic or linguistic background, no matter your political allegiances, I hope this book makes you question some of your beliefs and notice some of our collective blind spots—and that it opens your heart to other possibilities, other realities, and other opportunities to do things a little differently.

To every immigrant who leaves what they've known behind searching for a new home, a new start, and new dreams, I hope your landing will be soft and the welcome kind. To all the second and third-generation kids like me, I see you. You *are* home.

Bibliography

Beaudoin-Bégin, Anne-Marie. *La Langue Rapaillée: Combattre l'Insécurité Linguistique des Québécois.* Montréal: Éditions Somme toute, 2015.

Boucher, Francis. *La Grande Déception.* Montreal: Éditions Somme toute, 2018.

Cardinal, Mario. *Breaking Point Quebec—Canada: The 1995 Referendum.* Montréal: Bayard Canada Livres, 2005.

Cavafy, Constantine P. *Waiting for the Barbarians, Collected Poems,* trans. Edmund Keeley and Philip Sherrard. Princeton: Princeton University Press, 1975.

Choudhury, Shakil. *Deep Diversity: Overcoming Us vs. Them.* Toronto: Between the Lines, 2015.

Conradi Alexa. *Les angles mortes: Perspectives sur le Québec actuel.* Montréal: Les Éditions du remue-ménage, 2017.

Corneiller, Bruno. "The Struggle of Others: Pierre Vallières, Québécois Settler Nationalism, and the N-Word Today," *Discourse: Journal for Theoretical Studies in Media and Culture,* 39, no. 1, 2017.

Dawson, Caroline. *Là où je me terre.* Montréal: Les Éditions du remue-ménage, 2020.

Dodge, William, ed., transl. Christopher Korchin. *Boundaries of Identity: A Quebec Reader.* Toronto: Lester Publishing Limited, 1992.

Glaude Jr., Eddie S. *Begin Again: James Baldwin's America and Its Urgent Lessons for Our Own*. New York: Crown, 2020.

Goodman, Adam. *The Deportation Machine*. Princeton: Princeton University Press, 2020.

Hébert, Paul C. "A Microcosm of the General Struggle," in *Black Thought and Activism in Montreal, 1960-1969*. Doctoral thesis, University of Michigan, 2015.

Karmis, Dimitrios. « Un couteau reste un couteau? Réflexions sur les limites de l'hospitalité québécoise. » *Du tricoté serré au métissé serré? La culture publique commune au Québec en débats*. Sainte-Foy : Les Presses de l'Université Laval, 2008.

Lalonde, Michèle. *Speak White*. Montréal: Les Éditions de l'Hexagone, 1974.

Lubrano, Alfred. *Limbo: Blue-Collar Roots, White-Collar Dreams*. Hoboken: Wiley, 2005.

Memmi, Albert. *Racism*. Minneapolis: University of Minnesota Press,1999.

Micone, Marco. *Speak What*. Montréal: VLB éditeur, 2001.

Morand, Geneviève and Roy Natalie-Ann, eds. *Libérer la colère*. Montréal: Éditions Remue-Ménage, 2018.

Moscrop, David. *Too Dumb for Democracy? Why We Make Bad Political Decisions and How We Can Make Better Ones*. Fredericton: Goose Lane Editions, 2019.

Nayeri, Dina. *The Ungrateful Refugee: What Immigrants Never Tell You*. Berkeley: Catapult, 2019.

Pires, Rosa. « Décoloniser le « nous » de la gauche souverainiste », *Nouveaux Cahiers du socialisme*, (15). 2016.

Pires, Rosa. *Ne Sommes-Nous Pas Québécoises*. Montréal: Éditions du remue-ménage, 2019.

Richler, Mordecai. *Oh Canada, Oh Quebec: Requiem for a Divided Country*. Toronto: Penguin Books, 1992.

Rifaat, Cherif. *Immigrants Adapt, Countries Adopt. Or Not: Fitting into the Cultural Mosaic*. New Canadians Press, 2003.

Rushdie, Salman. "Imaginary Homelands," London Review of Books, October 7, 1982.

Saad, Layla F. *Me and White Supremacy*. Illinois: Sourcebooks, 2020.

Saint-Éloi, Rodney. « Un soir d'exile », *Nouvelles de Montréal*. Paris: Éditions Magellan & Cie, 2018.

Seymour, Michel. *Raison, Déraison, et Religion: Plaidoyer pour une laïcité ouverte*. Montréal: Écosociété, 2021.

Tan, Amy. "Mother Tongue," *The Threepenny Review*, No. 43. Autumn, 1990.

Verboczy, Akos, trans. Casey Roberts. *Rhapsody in Quebec: On the Path of an Immigrant Child*. Montreal: Baraka Books, 2017.

Williams, Ian. *Disorientation: Being Black in the World*. Toronto: Random House Canada, 2021.

Zubrzycki, Geneviève. *Beheading the Saint: Nationalism, Religion, And Secularism in Quebec*. Chicago: University of Chicago Press, 2016.